D1437129

Sir Robert Borden

Sir Robert Borden
Canada

Martin Thornton

First published in Great Britain in 2010 by
Haus Publishing Ltd
70 Cadogan Place
London SW1X 9AH
www.hauspublishing.com

A CIP catalogue record for this book
is available from the British Library

ISBN 978-1-905791-84-2

Series design by Susan Buchanan
Typeset in Sabon by MacGuru Ltd
Printed in Dubai by Oriental Press

Contents

Acknowledgements vii
Preface ix

I The Life and the Land 1
1 The Coming of Age of Canada 3
2 Development of a Future Leader 16
3 Prime Minister Robert Borden 28

II The Paris Peace Conference 37
4 Rough Road to Versailles: the First World War and the Planning for Peace 39
5 Anglo-Canadian relations at Versailles 61

III The Legacy 95
6 The Early Post-war Years 97
7 Final Years: the Aftermath of the Peace Conferences 122
8 Peace and War: Canada's Place in World Affairs 134
9 Conclusion 144

Notes 148
Chronology 162
Further Reading and Bibliography 172
Picture Sources 182
Index 185

Dedication

For the Quanes: Eileen Marie Quane Thornton,
Sean Lawrence Quane Thornton and
Ethan David Quane Thornton

Acknowledgements

The National Archives of Canada in Ottawa have been very helpful as ever in directing me to the appropriate material on Sir Robert Borden, their photocopies and reproduction service providing photocopies of the relevant microfilm. As most researchers know, microfilm was designed for those who have no interest in being able to read documents and have a spare lifetime. Despite many photographic references being on-line, I always find the old card index of photographs at the National Archives a nice distraction. Sir Robert Borden was President of the Canadian Historical Association and could be justifiably proud of the services that the National Archives provide for historians.

Although the service is as excellent, the small room of the House of Lords Archive that serves as a reading room for David Lloyd George's Papers contrasts with the rather large reading room of the National Archives in Canada. For the help provided in both, I am grateful.

The University of Leeds' Brotherton Library has been a depository of Canadian Government material for the past thirty years and has built up an excellent collection of Canadian material. Much of the microfilm resources are gradually being replaced by digital resources. Much of the Canadian material in the Brotherton Library has been purchased with financial support of the Department of Foreign Affairs and International Trade of the Canadian Government. Chapter 5 has been given as a conference paper at the British Association of Canadian Studies at St Anne's College, Oxford, in March 2009.

My sons, Sean and Ethan, have helped me find some small details as they manage to navigate the Internet more easily than I can. One of my sons found the topic surprisingly interesting, although neither of them study History. My wife has read many of my academic pieces of work on Canada and for that there should be a medal.

My final acknowledgement is to the publishers, who have had the imagination and largesse to harness a considerable amount of historical work on individuals and countries related to the peace conferences of 1919–23 and publish them in the form of a very substantial series.

Martin Thornton

University of Leeds

Preface

There are very few anecdotes of Sir Robert Laird Borden. Those anecdotes that do exist are rather undistinguished and not entirely revealing. This gives the impression of a rather plodding, moody and dismissive character; a view not entirely improved by the reading of the two volumes of his *Memoirs*, which despite some excellent and interesting detail, are rather restrained. One anecdote recounts Borden at the Ottawa golf club, where he was heard addressing the golf ball and himself before teeing off: *Now Borden, God damn you, keep your fool head down.*[1] This is a rare account of him using strong language, but indicative of the fact that he drove himself very hard. In politics, he did not keep his head down, even if it took persuasion to get him into a public arena where he could face an electorate. He had to put his head above the parapet to debate the great political issues of his age, and his character was severely tested in leading Canada during the First World War. He should, however, be remembered for his contributions toward a hard-won peace and the legacy of this peace for Canada and the Commonwealth.

Sir Robert Borden's head, with its full white mane of hair and bristling moustache, makes him arguably one of the more attractive figures in Sir William Orpen's painting, *Peace Conference at the Quai d'Orsay,* shown on the back cover of this book; and although he is tucked away in the right hand corner, he still appears a prominent personage. Historian John English suggested his image reflected an earlier period of history: 'In photographs of wartime and later, Borden seems to belong to an earlier age: he wears Edwardian suits and watch chains and parts his hair in the middle.' [2] Of course, he was Edwardian in an Edwardian age, but he might have appeared slightly anachronistic by the end of the First World War. It is a good job he is in the painting *Peace Conference at the Quai d'Orsay*, since he is quite rightly not in the companion painting by Sir William Orpen, *The Signing of Peace in the Hall of Mirrors, Versailles, 28th June 1919*, used on the endpapers. That is an interesting story in itself. Borden did not stay to sign the Peace Treaty and ancillary treaties on behalf of Canada; this was left to Charles Doherty and Arthur Sifton. Sir Robert Borden left Paris on 14 May 1919, feeling that his time could be better spent in Ottawa adding needed leadership to his Unionist Government. In Orpen's painting, held at the Imperial War Museum in London, it is Sir George Foster who is represented. Historian Charles Stacey points out: 'Canada is represented by the long solemn features and picturesque white beard of Sir George Foster, who wasn't there.'[3] He is in the group in the left corner, to the left of M Nikola Pašić of Serbia who has the longest beard in the painting. Foster was not there at the signing because he returned to Canada to be with his wife who was ill and died on 17 September 1919.

The absence of Borden from this prominent painting of the signing of the Peace Treaty should not distract us from the importance of Borden in the peace conferences of 1919–23 and their aftermath. The signing of the treaty by Canada was far more important to Borden than his personal presence.

ooooo

Sir Robert Laird Borden, born in Nova Scotia, lived from 1854 to 1937 and was the eighth Prime Minister of Canada since Canadian Confederation in 1867. He served as a Conservative Prime Minister from 10 October 1911 to 12 October 1917 and as Prime Minister of a Unionist Government from 12 October 1917 to 10 July 1920.[4] He had a swift rise through Conservative Party politics to become leader of the Opposition Party in Parliament, and this ultimately led to his becoming Prime Minister in 1911. He is remembered as a long-serving Prime Minister in a tumultuous period of domestic and international history for Canada.

On a domestic front, Borden is associated with introducing income tax in Canada in 1917 (presented initially as a temporary measure) and a controversial Wartime Elections Act of 20 September 1917, that among other things gave female relatives of Canadian and British forces personnel the vote and enhanced Borden's chances of securing a Unionist Government victory in the general election that followed. Universal suffrage itself followed on 24 May 1918 by extending the franchise to women over the age of 21 to vote in federal elections (with some property qualifications still existing in some Provinces).

Sir Robert Borden has found recognition within Canada, with his appearance on the $100 dollar bill and on postage stamps, with statutes commemorating him and schools named after him. Rather surprisingly, he has a town with few distinguishing characteristics named after him in Western Australia.

The view of Borden as the linchpin of Canada's new international autonomy is acknowledged in Borden's statue on Parliament Hill in Ottawa – a statue depicting Borden carrying a scroll that represents the Canadian brief he took to the Paris Peace Conference in 1919. Canadian Prime Minister Brian Mulroney wrote in the *Globe and Mail* in January 2002: 'There is a strong historical case to be made that if Sir John A Macdonald was the father of Canadian nationhood, Sir Robert Borden was the father of Canadian sovereignty.'[5]

Is Borden's reputation justified? The answer will be shown to be yes, but Borden is often seen as a marginal figure in histories of the Versailles settlements and peripheral to some memoir accounts of the period. Robert Borden addressed some of this neglect himself in providing coverage of events in his two volumes of *Memoirs*. A rather nice account of Borden's eye for historical recognition is found in his pique at not being included in an index for a multi-volume history of the Paris Peace Conference produced by the Royal Institute of International Affairs.[6]

Between 1912 and 1946, the Prime Minister was also the Secretary of State for External Affairs, a combination that gave him a very dominant position over foreign policy. However, I hope the impression given in this book is not that Robert Borden single-handedly put Canada on the world stage and developed Canadian foreign policy on his own. From the development of the Department of External Affairs in 1909 until 1941 two people held the position of Undersecretary of State for External Affairs, Sir Joseph Pope (from 1909 to 1925) and Dr O. D Skelton (from 1925 to 1941).[7] A figure that Borden relied on in drafting war aims for Canada and throughout visits to London and Paris during and after the First World War was another Nova Scotian, Loring

Cheney Christie, from Amherst, Nova Scotia. Borden and Christie went together to the Imperial War Conferences held in 1917 and 1918, to the Paris Peace Conference of 1919 and the Washington Naval Conference of 1921–2.

Sir Robert Borden is thus not the only subject of this book, and further key figures such as the Canadians Sir George E. Foster, Arthur Lewis Sifton, Arthur Meighen, William Lyon Mackenzie King, and Lester Bowles Pearson; the Britons David Lloyd George, Arthur James Balfour, Lord Robert Cecil, and Andrew Bonar Law; the South African General Jan Christian Smuts; the Americans Woodrow Wilson and Robert Lansing; and the French Premier Georges Clemenceau all make an appearance.

Sir Robert Borden a portrait photograph taken in 1920

I

The Life and the Land

1 The Coming of Age of Canada

Peoples of Canada

The population of Canada is made up of diverse ethnic groups derived from Aboriginal and non-Aboriginal people. Aboriginal people in Canada are officially defined as First Nations, Inuit and Métis. Métis has been used in Canada to describe people of mixed First Nation and European descent. Aboriginal people in Canada have occasionally had an impact on international affairs. The appeal of the Six Nations tribes of the Iroquois to the League of Nations in 1923 and 1924 is a case in point. Chief Deskaheh attempted to get the League of Nations to discuss grievances of the Six Nations. It ended in failure for the Six Nations since their legal claim to be represented at an international organisation had no obvious legal foundation, but it was a reminder to the world that people other than Europeans inhabited Canada, and that Canada was being rather tiresome in the League of Nations at the time about Article X of the Covenant (mutual undertaking to preserve and protect territorial sovereignty). The Six Nations obtained some brief support from the improbable sources of the Netherlands, Panama, Persia, Estonia and the Irish Free State.

European migration to Canada began in the early 17th century with French immigrants, but became dominated by British immigration into Canada in the 18th century. New France was a very large area of North America colonised by France until 1763. As a disjointed collection of colonies, it was British subjects who settled and dominated a sizeable area of North America. From 1608 until 1760 a French colony was in existence, to be followed by a British Crown Colony. Robert Borden, in a lecture to the University of Toronto in 1921, summarised the situation: *The French population which passed under British rule in 1760 comprised about 70,000 souls.*[1] The Treaty of Paris of 10 February 1763 relinquished Canada to the British, and it allowed for the liberty of the Catholic religion in Canada which was then followed by a proclamation setting the limits of Quebec.

Commonwealth historian John Miller points out: 'The central fact is that in the hundred years between the battle of Waterloo and the outbreak of World War 1 over 20 million people left the British Isles to migrate to countries beyond Europe, … four million went to Canada …'.[2] At the start of 1911 the population of Canada was 7,206,643; by 1921 it was 8,787,949; and in 1931 still only 10,376,786.[3] The slow growth is partly explained by emigration from Canada to the United States and also various restrictions that Canada attached to immigration, an area of foreign policy over which it had political control. Migrants often used Canada as a stepping stone to the United States, and any relative economic advantages that the United States was perceived to have over Canada meant labour often moved south. Two Immigration Acts of Parliament in 1906 and 1910 saw British immigrants favoured, with northern Europeans favoured over southern Europeans and immigrants from Asia seen as far less favourable. A most-favoured-nations approach was to be pursued in the inter-war years.

The census of 1911 is also interesting because 'There were 403,417 Canadians who identified themselves as German in the 1911 census, and 44,036 who were "Austrians" – about 6.2 per cent of the population.'[4] It is intriguing that Canada's attitude towards entering both world wars is couched in such a publicly strong commitment to support Britain, the 'mother country'. Of course the large British connection swept opposition aside, including some French indifference in Quebec where they might have been expected to more forcefully support their own 'mother country'.

Geography of Canada

In 1818 Britain and the United States agreed a land frontier between Canada and the United States. Starting from the east, the St Lawrence Seaway through the Great Lakes served as the boundary, with the 49th parallel being established as a dividing line from the Lake of the Woods up to the Rocky Mountains. By the Oregon Treaty of 1846 the border was extended further westwards to the coast. These arrangements had been helped by the Rush-Bagot Agreement of 1817 (Richard Rush was United States Secretary of State and Charles Bagot the British Minister to the United States) that regulated naval armaments of the British and the United States on the Great Lakes and Lake Champlain. From these developments Canada and the United States are often listed as having maintained the longest 'unmilitarised' border in the world.

On 15 March 1923, Sir Joseph Pope, Undersecretary of State for External Affairs of Canada, had reason to explain the geographical and special circumstances of Canada to Sir

Eric Drummond, the first Secretary General of the League of Nations. Their correspondence related to national security and the position of Canada in terms of Empire defence. Pope summarised the position of Canada: 'Canada with a population of 8,788, 483 and an area of 3,729,665 square miles has a land frontier including the shore of the Great Lakes of about 3,800 miles facing the United States of America, and a land frontier of about 1,500 miles facing Alaska (territory of the United States of America). It has several thousand miles of coast line on the Atlantic, the Arctic and the Pacific Oceans, with only a small naval force of its own.'[5] Given the size of the territorial waters of Canada, its navy at the time of the Washington Naval Conference in 1921 and early 1922 appeared decidedly modest, consisting of two destroyers, a cruiser and some auxiliary craft received from the British Government. Then, of course, who exactly was going to attack Canada?

Geography is a general determinant of a country's foreign policy and territorial disputes have a long association with the outbreak of wars. Canada has the special accolade of being the second largest country in the world and it shares the North American continent with a country more militarily and economically powerful than itself. It will be shown between 1919 and 1923 and beyond that geography has been a very significant element in Canada's attitudes towards Europe, the Paris settlements, naval disarmament and relations with the British Empire, other Dominions and the United States.

Confederation of Canada

The administration of Canada by the British in the late 18th and early 19th centuries was a division into Upper and Lower Canada and then as a Province from 1841. The Confederation of Canada itself did not take place until 1867, when the British North America Act, an Act of the British Parliament, provided a written constitution for an independent Canada. Much of Canadian history is presented as pre or post-Confederation history. Ontario, Quebec, Nova Scotia and New Brunswick were the founding provinces of Canada, followed by Manitoba (1870), British Columbia (1871), Prince Edward Island (1873), Alberta and Saskatchewan (1905) and Newfoundland (1949). With the Yukon and Northwest Territories, Canada comprised ten provinces and two territories. A greater amount of federal jurisdiction was applied to the territories. The Constitution Act of 1982, that saw the constitution of Canada 'patriated' from Britain, did not change this basic structure, and this was the situation until on the 1 April 1999 the self-governing area of Nunavut (Inuktitut for 'Our Land') was created out of the central and eastern parts of the Northwest Territories.

When I resided in Halifax, Nova Scotia, I was one thousand miles nearer to London than to Vancouver on our western coast. If you could pivot Canada upon its eastern seaboard it would cover the northern part of the Atlantic Ocean, the British Islands, Norway, Sweden, Denmark, Holland, Belgium, the northern part of France, the entire German Empire and a considerable portion of European Russia.[6]

ROBERT BORDEN, ROYAL COLONIAL INSTITUTE, LONDON, 10 JULY 1912

The eminent Canadian historian Jack Granatstein has written: 'Confederation in 1867 did not bring substantial new powers, and it certainly did not bring independence. Canada was the first federation in the British Empire and some Canadians undoubtedly saw great days coming on the international stage, but Britain still wielded enormous authority over Canadian foreign policy. The diplomatic unity of the empire dictated that London would speak for Canada in all matters of foreign policy.'[7] Perhaps the phrase 'in all matters' is a trifle too strong, since in foreign policy terms there existed a vagueness about Canada's international position; this remained unchanged in 1909 despite the creation of the small Department of External Affairs (for some years little more than a sorting office for correspondence between the British and Canadian governments). Granatstein continues: 'Britain was the mother country, and the other dominions were not foreigners but members of an imperial family. Hence the term "external affairs".'[8] Canada was not expected to have a different foreign policy from the British Empire, and for that matter, Canadians did not expect to have a different foreign policy from Great Britain on issues that related to the Empire.

This relationship was very much in existence up to and including much of the First World War. Although commercial policies had led to some bilateral agreements between Canada and other countries, the basic situation reflecting Canada's lack of international standing had not changed. A sea change (if you can excuse the pun) was not that evident when Robert Borden tried to influence imperial naval policy from 1912, but became clearer towards the end of the First World War. Although Canada had a French-Canadian prime minister, Sir Wilfrid Laurier, from 1896 to 1911, this did not manifestly change the circumstances of Canada's relationship with Great Britain. Laurier was aware of the strong Anglo-Saxon links of the Canadian population and was also personally enamoured by the nature of the British Empire and the British traditions that helped to define Canada; he was happy to be knighted, and consequently, could be considered pro-British.

The size and geographic position of Canada meant that

it largely had no expansionist ambitions for its territory. Furthermore, for a substantial number of Canadians there was no particular association with the sea. However, given the fact that Canada borders three major oceans (Atlantic, Pacific and Arctic), its interest in the laws of the sea and the protection of trade routes was paramount. Canada's war aims might be seen to be the protection of the trade routes of the North Atlantic, but for both the First and Second World Wars Canada's aims were presented in the most general terms, emphasising the protection of civilization and the importance of the rule of law. Legal and rational approaches to foreign policy and the interpretation of the international system were as evident at the beginning of the First World War as they are now.

One historian said of the First World War that it 'brought Canadians to Europe, but left Europe remote to Canadians'[9] while French-Canadian Senator Raoul Dandurand said, in 1924, that Canada was 'a fire proof house far from inflammable materials'.[10] These views partly explain Canada's own form of isolationism in the inter-war years. Although Canadian isolationism would parallel that in the United States in trying to avoid entangling alliances, it would also try to avoid commitments within the British Empire and the League of Nations that might force Canada into conflicts against her considered welfare.

Since Canada had been a colony and only obtained independence in 1867 (a qualified independence at that), Canada had moved slowly to be a nation, and by 1919 was still trying to establish her independence in foreign policy. Robert MacGregor Dawson describes the constitutional position of the Dominions, Canada, Australia, South Africa, New Zealand and Newfoundland (the Irish Free State became the sixth

Dominion on 6 December 1921) in the years 1920–22 as 'The Period of Tentative Centralization'. This is a period when it was still possible to suggest that a common foreign policy existed for the British Empire and Dominions. This was swiftly followed by 1922–26, 'The Period of Decentralization,' as the Chanak Crisis related to Turkey and the Locarno Pacts in Europe exposed the lack of a common foreign policy.[11]

Canada could rightly claim to be the largest and oldest Dominion, and at the Paris Peace Conference it was not looking to be a colonial power or to protect any colonies. In fact, the British Prime Minister, Lloyd George, was surprised during the Conference that Sir Robert Borden turned down the opportunity to have Canada administer the British West Indies. This was remembered by Lloyd George as a rejection because of what he considered to be a North American malady. 'Canada has no tropical or semi-tropical territory, and I thought the undertaking might interest the Canadian people. I found that Sir Robert Borden was deeply imbued with the American prejudice against the government of extraneous possessions and peoples which did not form an integral part of their own Union. He therefore gave no encouragement to my suggestion, and I dropped it.'[12]

Any interests shown by Canada in helping to administer or dominate areas like Greenland (Danish), Alaska (American), West Indies (British), St Pierre and Miquelon (French) or Newfoundland (independent) could be seen as half-hearted and not taken seriously. This was the case until Newfoundland's bankruptcy led them to join the Dominion of Canada in 1949. Otherwise, Canada had no territorial ambitions in 1919 and supported President Woodrow Wilson's views on captured territory and colonies; that if a security issue did not prevail, particularly for the British Empire, the captured territory should be under the mandate of the League of Nations.

Canada's political relationships with the United States and Great Britain contrast in interesting ways. The Canadian Government found it possible to operate with Great Britain and the United States in a North Atlantic Triangle, and although the North Atlantic Triangle description has been applied to the early post-Second World War years, it can also be seen to be evident in the inter-war years. Canada could not ignore the United States, and the Prime Minister of Canada, Mackenzie King, emphasised this in October 1923: 'We are right alongside a vast continent with which we have to compete in every particular. Geographically we are handicapped in that competition all along the way. Our winters make it more difficult for our railways to operate, our seasons are not as long or as varied as the seasons of the country to the south of us, and we have the handicap of a smaller population.'[13] Yet Canada maintained very friendly relations with the United States and found at different times the benefits of trade with the country. Equally, at other times, the problems of trading with the United States and the British Empire caused political frictions, and periods of economic protectionism would occur.

Canada's place in international law

The story of Canadian foreign policy autonomy is also a story about the transition of the Dominions towards a Commonwealth of Nations. Prior to the First World War, the position of Canada as an international entity was clear to some lawyers. One suggestion was that within international law the Dominions were clearly part of the mother country. Sir Robert Borden's favourite legal source for international law in 1921 was Lassa Oppenheim.

He was to make a strong point about the Dominions before the First World War: 'It did not matter that some of them, as for example, Canada and Australia, flew as their own flag the modified flag of the mother country, or that they had their own coinage, their own postage stamps, and the like. Nor did they become subjects of International Law (although the position was somewhat anomalous) when they were admitted, side by side with the mother country, as parties to the administrative unions, such as the Universal Postal Union.' [14] These were minor trappings of independence, but the political relationship between Canada and the 'mother country', Great Britain, which favoured the 'mother country', was paramount in important foreign policy areas.

Lassa F L Oppenheim (1858–1919) is often portrayed as the father of the discipline of international law. His *International Law: A Treatise, Volume 1, Peace* (1905) and *Volume 2, War and Neutrality* (1906) have become textbooks that have been re-edited by further scholars into many editions. Oppenheim was a German scholar who moved to England in 1895, becoming in 1908 Whewell Professor of International Law at the University of Cambridge, where he died in October 1919. He was a believer in the supremacy of national sovereignty over international law, but was a strong advocate of the League of Nations, and lectured on the topic shortly before his death. In 1919 Oppenheim reworked parts of his famous two-volume *International Law* for a third edition, and this was used and footnoted by Borden in his Marfleet Lectures of 1921.

The above was seriously challenged during and immediately after the First World War, when at the Paris Peace Conference of 1919 the Dominions and India were represented individually within the British Empire delegation, and were founding members of the League of Nations. After the Paris Conference, the Dominions were individually represented in the Assembly of the League and could vote there independently of Great Britain. Oppenheim was to attempt to clarify the situation further: 'Without doubt, therefore, the admission of these four self-governing Dominions [Australia, Canada, South Africa and New Zealand] within the family of Nations at present defies exact definition, since they enjoy a special position corresponding to their special status within the British Empire as "free communities, independent as regards all their own affairs, and partners in those which concern the Empire at large."'[15] The only thing that becomes clear from the point of international law was that the situation had not been made transparently clear as a consequence of the Paris Peace Conference.

Commonwealth

In turn, the notion of a Commonwealth has not always been defined clearly. The historical derivation of the word is linked to two words, 'common weal', meaning common good or community welfare. References to a commonwealth as a body politic or political community can be found in the 14th century, and became popular when applied to the Republican Government after the execution of King Charles I in 1649. The word was prominently used by the political theorist and philosopher Thomas Hobbes in *Leviathan* (1651), and the prominence of the term 'a commonwealth of nations' as a group of states is evident in the work of Edmund Burke, the notable British statesman and philosopher in the late 18th century. In the 19th century, the term commonwealth gets used intermittently to describe the colonial empire of Great Britain. By 1907, the term Dominion was employed in government circles to differentiate between the self-governing colonies (for example: Australia, Canada and New Zealand) and India and the Crown colonies, where the administration and legislature were controlled by the Crown (for example:

Bermuda, Jamaica and Ceylon). Not surprisingly, Britain and the Dominions could be seen as a commonwealth or community of nations, and they were described freely as such. William David McIntyre lists the books of Lionel Curtis (author and British public servant) as popularising the phrase 'British Commonwealth of Nations' in his 1914 book *The Commonwealth of Nations* and in the 1916 publication, *The Problem of the Commonwealth*.[16] In a famous resolution to the Imperial War Conference of 1917, put forward by Sir Robert Borden, the *autonomous nature of an Imperial Commonwealth* was mentioned.[17] Borden also pronounced in his Marfleet Lectures of 1921: *The British Commonwealth embraces five self-governing nations...* .[18] Clearly, the term British Commonwealth was being used before the Statute of Westminster in 1931, a statute that legally defines the British Commonwealth of Nations.

The First World War created some disillusion between the Dominions and the 'mother country'. The Dominions emerged with a growing self-confidence and with new ambitions to be involved in British Empire decision-making when they believed it affected them. However, it took the important Balfour Declaration on Dominion status in 1926 (not to be confused with the Balfour Declaration on Palestine from 1917) to give us the definition of a very specific organisation of states called the 'British Commonwealth of Nations' or 'Commonwealth'. The latter title is favoured after the Second World War with the independence of Asian states and later African states that chose freely to join the Commonwealth.

Canada has been fortunate to have some long-serving and respected Prime Ministers. Prime Minister of Canada for nearly nine years from 1911 to 1920, Sir Robert Laird Borden is associated with helping to establish international recognition for Canada and helping Canada become recognised as a sovereign nation. This was partly achieved by Borden in winning a voice for Canada in the Allied peace negotiations in Paris after the First World War. Dominion autonomy, it is argued, was fashioned by obtaining representation for Canada and other British Dominions in the League of Nations and the International Labour Organisation.[19] Historians have pointed out that it was the Paris Peace Conference that brought Canadian representatives into substantial diplomatic contact with other nations around the world and provided a new form of diplomatic interaction for them.[20] Through membership of the League of Nations, Canada was to find itself involved in a new intercourse with the world that went beyond its normal relations with the British Empire and the United States. Although it will be seen that Canada's role in the 1919 Peace Conference was limited in practical terms, the general feeling among Canadians that they were now concerning themselves with high policy issues was significant. Membership of the League of Nations also appeared to bring with it new obligations and commitments.

A qualifying consideration to the above is that despite the opportunities for diplomatic influence at the League of Nations before 1925, Canada had little in the way of government offices abroad, only the 'High Commissioner's office in London and the Commissioner General's office in Paris'.[21] It was the British who provided consular and diplomatic means of communication for Canada. 'The First Canadian legation was opened in Washington in 1927, followed by Paris in 1928 (replacing the Commissioner General's office), and Tokyo in 1929. No other Canadian diplomatic offices were opened until 1939.'[22]

2

Development of a Future Leader

As his name might suggest, Sir Robert Laird Borden was descended from ancestors in Scotland and England. On his father's side he could trace his ancestry to a man from Kent in England from about 1370 and his much later descendant Richard Borden, who emigrated to New England in 1638. It was one of Richard's descendants who relocated to Nova Scotia as a United Empire Loyalist (those who retained some loyalty to the British Empire). His mother's relatives included emigrants from Scotland; her grandfather, Robert Laird, emigrated to Nova Scotia via Ireland and New England. Sir Robert Borden could also trace a maternal great-grandfather who resided in New Haven, Connecticut, but whose family appeared to derive from the East Riding of Yorkshire in England.[1]

Robert Borden's character was the product of the strong influences of his family, his locality (notably a farming community in Nova Scotia), a Presbyterian Sunday school, and the experience of teaching others and eventually studying law. Law became his road into politics, and it was his friendships and legal reputation that advanced him into a political career. He had a stern moral character that suited the politics of his age.

Borden was not unlike a number of other successful Canadian political figures in having his religious upbringing influence his general ideological beliefs. Among a group of eminent future members of the Canadian Department of External Affairs were four whose fathers were clergymen: Lester Pearson (also to be Prime Minister), Arnold Heeney, Escott Reid and Hume Wrong.[2] It was not that they were particularly religious, but they had strong Protestant moral values to draw upon in dealing with Canadian foreign policy during their prominent careers. The high moral values Borden retained influenced his management of Canadian foreign policy and views of Canada's position in the world.

Robert Borden was the final Canadian Prime Minister to have been born before Confederation. He was born in Grand Pré, Nova Scotia on 26 June 1854, the son of Andrew Borden and Eunice Jane Laird (who had married in 1850). Andrew Borden was a farmer, but due to limited business success became the station-master at Grand Pré for the Windsor-Annapolis Railway Company.[3] His first marriage was to Catherine Fuller, and this marriage produced two children, Thomas and Sophie. His first wife died in 1847, and with his second wife, Eunice, Andrew had four children, Robert, John, Julia and Henry (or Hal as he was known).[4] It was Eunice Borden who was a particularly powerful influence on her eldest son Robert, encouraging his interest in literature and languages. From Robert's own description it would appear that his character most resembled that of his mother: *She had very keen likes and dislikes and, although she was of remarkably vigorous physique, had a highly-wrought nervous temperament. She was passionate but wholly just and considerate upon reflection.*[5] His mother was Presbyterian, hence he attended the local Presbyterian Sunday school; but he also occasionally attended the local Anglican church to which his father belonged. Although born on a farm and part of a small farming community, and a boy who by all accounts worked hard at his chores, his life was not entirely that of a pioneer. Robert's education was not neglected, and he developed a love of classical literature. In 1863 he was sent to a local private school, Acacia Villa, and rose rather swiftly to be an assistant teacher there when he was only fourteen years old. It is hardly surprising that he began to take life rather seriously, but his serious demeanour and love of the classics would serve him well through life. After four further years he moved to Matawan, New Jersey in the United States to help teach at the Glenwood Institute, teaching mostly classics and mathematics. This move did not entirely separate him from his family; his married half-brother lived not too far away in New York.[6]

Although teaching provided a potential opportunity for a long term career, Robert found the prospect unfulfilling, and looked to the legal profession as a more rewarding prospect and for financial security. The Province of Ontario, with Ottawa as the seat of the federal government, was an obvious area for ambitious lawyers, but Robert's family encouraged him to choose Nova Scotia. Regardless of not having a university degree, he became an articled clerk for Weatherbe and Graham, a law firm in Halifax, and in 1878 was admitted to the Bar of Nova Scotia. Despite not having formal legal training or a law degree, he managed to come top of his competitive class list and proved the virtues of self-education. *Like other law students of the day, I worked laboriously in the office from nine a.m. until six p.m., receiving a trifling remuneration for keeping the account books. In the evenings one occupied oneself in endeavouring to master, as best one could, the mysteries of the Law. There was no law school in Nova Scotia at the time ... .*[7] Interestingly, as Borden's principal biographer Robert Craig Brown footnotes, in 1881 there were some 245 barristers in Nova Scotia, although this is described as 'small'.[8]

It was in Halifax that Robert developed military interests, and in his spare time became a member of the Halifax Volunteers, 63rd Battalion of Rifles and went to a school of military instruction in the evenings. A minor diversion in the garrison town of Halifax in the summer was the arrival of a fleet of ships, an event about which Borden sounds rather prudish and even censorious: *The influence of the garrison and the navy upon young men was not wholesome as they were led to emulate the leisure of military and naval officers.*[9] More to his liking were occasional visits from his family, particularly his mother, Hal, Sophie, and Julia.

New Conservative Party political contacts arrived as he began working in association with a law firm in Kentville as a junior partner with John P Chipman, but the attraction of moving back to Halifax and a more prestigious company proved to be too great. He joined his old mentor Wallace Graham alongside Charles Hibbert Tupper (son of prominent Conservative politician, Sir Charles Tupper) as a junior partner in 1882. Charles Hibbert Tupper was elected a Member of Parliament for Pictou in that year. Working assiduously on Government causes, including American-Canadian fishing rights problems, introduced Borden to international and Canadian political issues, and led to appearances before the Supreme Court of Canada. Borden could be seen as fortunate as he was now able to develop contacts in Ottawa that included Prime Minister Sir John Thompson and Charles Hibbert Tupper. Wallace Graham was on the Supreme Court of Nova Scotia, and in May 1888 Charles Hibbert Tupper was made Minister of Marines and Fisheries. The workload for Robert Borden was immense,[10] but in 1889 he became the senior partner in Graham and Tupper. The name of Tupper was later dropped from the law firm, as under the leadership of Borden, the firm developed with new associates and became Borden, Ritchie, Parker and Chisholm, with work for the Justice Department covered by Graham, Borden and Parker.[11]

A dominant period for the politicians of Nova Scotia developed as three Prime Ministers came from the province. Borden was to be the third from Nova Scotia, after Sir John Thompson, Conservative Prime Minister, 5 December 1892 to 12 December 1894 and Sir Charles Tupper, Conservative Prime Minister, 1 May 1896 to 8 July 1896.

Robert Borden's life was not entirely dedicated to the law, however; he married Laura Bond in 1889. Borden explains the engagement and marriage in one sentence in his *Memoirs*, so we know little of his courtship or any excitement that might have accompanied the marriage.[12] She was a strong-willed individual also from Nova Scotia, her parents having a hardware business in Halifax. Laura and Robert, we do know, shared interests in literature and sport, particularly golf. The couple also shared a common delight in touring abroad, travelling throughout Europe in 1891, 1893 and 1895. The first visits to England and France by Borden had been in 1888.[13] In 1895, Borden went to England, accompanied by his wife, to appear before a delayed meeting of the Judicial Committee of the Privy Council; and it was this high level of public speaking, despite Borden's dislike of it, that prepared him for a political career.[14]

Robert and Laura's marriage was childless, but they always

showed an interest in the education and careers of relatives. Even in retirement, Robert Borden took on the financial responsibility for the education of his younger brother Hal's three children, after his brother was taken ill. The two volumes of Robert Borden's *Memoirs* were edited by his nephew, Henry Borden, Hal's son. How affectionate Robert was towards his family is not entirely clear, but he was close to his brother Hal and admired the academic talent of Henry.

Sir Charles Hibbert Tupper (1855–1927) was born in Amherst, Nova Scotia, the second son of Sir Charles Tupper, Prime Minister of Canada, 1 May 1896 to 5 February 1901. Charles Hibbert Tupper was Member of Parliament for Pictou, Nova Scotia from 1882 until his retirement from politics in 1904. He was also Minister of Marine and Fisheries 1888–94, Minister of Justice 1894–6, and briefly Solicitor General of Canada in 1896. Tupper and Borden were friends for years, despite Tupper moving to British Columbia, but their relationship deteriorated over Borden ignoring Tupper's suggestions for political appointments and during the First World War when Tupper's son died at Vimy Ridge in 1917. Tupper felt his son had been overlooked for promotion. Tupper also opposed Canada signing the Versailles Treaty independently of Great Britain.

It was the Conservative Party leader, Sir Charles Tupper (who was not only the father of Robert Borden's close friend, Charles Hibbert Tupper, but also a previous Premier of Nova Scotia) who suggested to Robert that he should run for the Canadian Parliament, representing Halifax. Notwithstanding the fact he had not previously expressed any obvious strong interest in political office, Borden accepted. What political views Robert Borden harboured seem to have been the Liberal Party views of his early years that were common in the Annapolis Valley of Nova Scotia. Most of his legal contemporaries gave their support to the Conservative Party, and these were the circles in which he moved. The Liberal Party's approach to what was seen as unrestricted trade reciprocity annoyed Borden. His successful nomination was followed by his election for the Conservative Party in 1896; an election that coincided with the Liberals forming a Government led by Wilfrid Laurier.

Early backbench life for Borden was not particularly eventful, doing the normal work of defending the interests of constituents and becoming involved in committees; the latter was an area in which he had some flair. One of the big economic and political issues of 1897 that Borden was to play a small role in during debates in the House of Commons was the issue of preferential trade with Britain. The circumstances of the debate exposed Borden to the broad issue of treaties within the British Empire and the self-governing colonies. The Laurier Government introduced a tariff allowing preferential treatment for Great Britain, believing they could give this preference to Britain alone. However, Great Britain had treaties with Germany and Belgium which stipulated their products would not be subject to higher tariffs than those from the colonies and possessions of Great Britain. Germany and Belgium would thus be entitled to the same preferred tariff from Canada that Canada offered to Britain. Further, the question arose as to whether, given the 'most favoured nation clause' of treaties that mentioned British possessions, preference would have to be given by Canada to nearly every nation in the world. Borden believed that it would, and argued thus in the House of Commons.

The conclusion of all this was a general 'denunciation' from a Colonial Conference: 'That the Premiers of the self-governing Colonies unanimously recommend the denunciation, at the earliest convenient time, of any treaties which now hamper the commercial relations between Great Britain and her Colonies.'[15] The treaties with Germany and Belgium were to cease within a year, but Great Britain also made special arrangements for Germany with regard to trade with Canada. The situation led Canada to put a further tax on German goods until more acceptable arrangements between Germany and Canada were agreed.

An interesting development of this was a poem, by that poet of Empire Rudyard Kipling, published in *The Times* of London on 27 April 1897: 'Our Lady of the Snows'. Prime Minister Laurier went on to use lines from the first stanza of the poem on more than one occasion to make a case for supporting the 'mother country'. Among these were debates in the House of Commons on the Boer War in 1900 and on the Naval Service Bill in 1910. Borden in his *Memoirs* includes the quotation from the imperial poet as cited by Laurier. It was a poem ostensibly concerned with Canada's decision to favour trade with Great Britain, but also to support Britain over the United States in a boundary dispute between Venezuela and British Guyana. Kipling evokes the English nationalism evident in the Canadian House of Commons at the time. Like much poetry it reflects a number of images that have had further relevance, in this case for Canada in the 20th century: Catholic Quebec, Empire issues, Canadian nationalism, Anglo-Canadian relations and the call to arms. It is not entirely timeless – probably the opposite – but it carried some resonance for Laurier and Borden.

'I claim for Canada this, that, in future Canada shall be at liberty to act or not act, to interfere or not interfere, to do just as she pleases, and that she shall reserve to herself the right to judge whether or not there is cause for her to act.'[16]

SIR WILFRID LAURIER, CANADIAN HOUSE OF COMMONS DEBATE, 5 FEBRUARY 1900

Being a backbencher in the opposition party and continuing to practise law did Borden no harm. Within three years

'OUR LADY OF THE SNOWS' BY RUDYARD KIPLING
'Last, but not least (he said), we give to the people the benefits of preferential trade with the mother-country.' – New Canadian Tariff

A nation spoke to a nation,
A Queen sent word to a Throne:–
'Daughter am I in my mother's house,
But mistress in my own.
The gates are mine to open,
As the gates are mine to close,
And I set my house in order,'
Said our Lady of the Snows.

'Neither with laughter nor weeping,
Fear or the child's amaze—
Soberly under the White Man's law
My white men go their ways.
Not for the Gentiles' clamour—
Insult or threat of blows—
Bow we the knee to Baal,'
Said our Lady of the Snows.

'My speech is clean and single,
I talk of common things—
Words of the wharf and the market-place
And the ware the merchant brings:
Favour to those I favour,
But a stumbling-block to my foes.
Many there be that hate us,'
Said our Lady of the Snows.

'I called my chiefs to council
In the din of a troubled year;
For the sake of a sign ye would not see,
And a word ye would not hear.
This is our message and answer;
This is the path we chose:
For we be also a people,'
Said our Lady of the Snows.

'Carry the word to my sisters—
To the Queens of the East and the South.
I have proven faith in the Heritage
By more than the word of the mouth.
They that are wise may follow
Ere the world's war-trumpet blows:
But I—I am first in the battle,'
Said our Lady of the Snows.

A Nation spoke to a Nation
A Throne sent word to a Throne:
'Daughter am I in my mother's house
But mistress in my own.
The gates are mine to open,
As the gates are mine to close,
And I abide by my Mother's House,'
Said our Lady of the Snows.

his loyalty to Sir Charles Tupper was rewarded with front bench representation for his political party in the House of Commons. Borden had managed to accumulate friends and political status in Ottawa, and the notoriety of being in the public gaze was something he was coming to enjoy.

Good fortune tends to favour the rise of many politicians and this, coupled with more obvious candidates for high office (George Eulas Foster and Charles Hibbert Tupper) cancelling each other out, led to Borden being asked to lead the

Conservative Party.[17] Within five years he went from being a novice Member of Parliament to leading the Conservatives, a meteoric and not easily politically justified elevation, except that he had few enemies. As he was to express to his close friend Charles Hibbert Tupper: *I have not either the experience or the qualifications which would enable me to successfully lead the party.*[18] Despite Borden's own expectation that he would lead the Conservative Party for only a year, he was to be in charge of his party for twenty years.

I have not either the experience or the qualifications which would enable me to successfully lead the party.

ROBERT BORDEN TO CHARLES HIBBERT TUPPER, 5 DECEMBER 1900

Borden's biographer, Robert Craig Brown, equivocates over whether or not Borden had discernible talents to lead his party: 'There was much to prove his success as a self-made man; there was little to suggest that he would be a successful leader of men. And yet, there was nothing to prove that he would not be or could not be a leader.'[19] Borden's mild wit and wisdom was evident when he took his seat in the House of Commons for the first time as leader of the Opposition. Sir Wilfrid Laurier took the opportunity to chide him: 'I am quite sure my honourable friend will believe in my sincerity when I tell him that I hope with all my heart he may continue to exercise for a long, long period the functions of Leader of the Opposition'.[20] Borden's retort included: *The right honourable gentleman will permit me to say, in passing, that if I should remain Leader of the Opposition for as long as that joke is old, it will be wholly beyond my own expectations, and beyond the expectations of the honourable gentlemen on this side of the House.*[21] He was showing that he had some capacity for leadership within the rough and tumble of parliamentary party politics, and even the occasional touch of dry wit.

A year after becoming leader of his party, Robert Borden toured the prairie and western provinces, areas of the country where he was not particularly well known and with which he was not familiar. The tour followed a particular formula of speeches and dinners with local dignitaries and, where possible, the introduction of local political issues. In British Columbia he pandered to local support for restricting immigrants from the Far East. His knowledge of British Columbia and this issue would be revisited in debates at the Paris Peace Conference in 1919. In referring to Chinese immigration in a speech at Winnipeg, Manitoba on 13 October 1902 at the end of his tour, he pandered to a rather populist opinion that related to British Columbia and the Chinese: *I am satisfied that they do not assimilate with the people of British Columbia; the people do not desire them to assimilate, and the Chinese do not desire to be assimilated … .*[22]

Robert Borden thought of resigning the Conservative Party leadership when he lost his electoral seat in the general election of 1904, as the Conservatives were trounced in Nova Scotia. However, he overcame this setback with a new seat in Carleton, Ontario in an uncontested election of 1905 (through the good graces of Wilfrid Laurier) and he continued to lead his Party. His dedication to the Conservative Party was also confirmed in 1905 when he gave up his law practice to concentrate on the interests and organisation of the Party. At least the Conservative Party performed better in the next general election in 1908; however, they did not defeat the Liberal Government. Borden was selected for constituencies in Carleton and Halifax, and chose to sit for Halifax.

Again, good fortune allowed him to serve as leader of the Opposition for ten years; the kind of political and administrative experience that would serve him well in the future.

He rose to public prominence without the serious worries of governing the nation. Borden's political style of leadership was to present logical arguments rather than flamboyant rhetoric, and this gave him the image of being plodding and unexciting. He felt some issues were above party politics, and this made him more of a consensus politician concerned with national interest. Robert Borden did not push for any substantial changes in imperial relationships when Canada joined in the Second Boer War in South Africa from 1899 to 1902. He understood the limitations of opposition and the premature nature of some national political strategies. Brown describes the gradualism of the imperial attitudes of Borden: 'It was of course, an evolving relationship, reflecting the growth of Canada to national maturity. The evolution would continue, would be gradual, and would be determined by circumstance. There would be no sudden change, force-fed by the elaborate theories and plans of Imperial centralists.'[23]

A great believer in self-government, Robert Borden took the general approach that imperial relationships derived from and were defined by this self-government. Borden did not wish, by imperial relationships, to limit Canada's ability to control its own affairs. He wished to contribute to a British Empire and Dominions foreign policy, but it was equally important that the Dominions helped to define the foreign policies of the Empire.

3 Prime Minister Robert Borden

Robert Borden's interest and involvement in imperial affairs was forced upon him by a naval crisis. Charles Stacey suggests that it was the naval issue that developed Borden's views on the position of the Dominions within the British Empire.[1] The limitations of Britain's naval strength against Germany had become apparent by 1909, and for Canada the naval question revolved around how Canada would contribute towards imperial defence. Naval rivalry between Germany and Great Britain focused on the building of capital ships. Should Canada have its own naval service, put Canadian ships at the disposal of an imperial navy or contribute in financial terms to an Imperial navy? French-Canadian politicians from Quebec queried the level of support Canada should be giving to Britain's imperial defence, wanting to reduce these commitments, or at least any commitments a long way from Canada. These questions were debated between and within the Canadian political parties. The defence of Canada was made a priority, with Canadian ships stationed off the Pacific and Atlantic coasts, ships that would be available to Great Britain should war break out.

It had been fourteen years since Robert Borden and his wife, Laura, visited England, but he took the time to do so from 29 June 1909, and they spent the next three months in Europe, arriving back in Ottawa on 1 October. Although he met with Canadian-born Andrew Bonar Law (future British Colonial Secretary, Chancellor of the Exchequer and Prime Minister) for the first time and made some speeches on Empire and naval security, the trip was largely uneventful from a political point of view.

In Canadian debates over the Naval Services Bill of 1910, memorable speeches were made by Sir Wilfrid Laurier and Robert Borden. Laurier expressed the strong statement that, 'When Britain is at war, Canada is at war; there is no distinction.'[2] Laurier was later to make a crucial qualification to these bold remarks, claiming that Canada would not necessarily participate in all the wars of Britain.[3] In turn, Borden evoked the evils of war and expressed his ideas in rather general terms, but he did nevertheless make it clear that he favoured an Imperial Defence Committee that would consult the Dominions before the outbreak of any substantial war. Borden's conclusions were not unlike those put forward by Laurier, pointing out in an unequivocal way and with some bravado: *When the battle of Armageddon comes, when the empire is fighting for its existence, when our kinsmen of the other great dominions are in the forefront of the battle, shall we sit silent and inactive while we contemplate with smug satisfaction our increasing crops and products, or, shall we pauper-like seek fancied but delusive security in an appeal to the charity of some indefinite and high-sounding political doctrine of a great neighbouring nation? No, a thousand times no.*[4]

After the grand debates about the protection of Empire,

the result was not considered of great significance; the Naval Service Act of 1910 established a Naval Service for Canada and the Department of the Naval Service.[5] However, the development of an independent Canadian navy under Prime Minister Laurier did not materialise; Canada would acquire two British cruisers for training naval personnel, rather than building its own. The construction of a Canadian fleet that would be a useful fighting force for the Empire was anticipated to take too long to build; possibly ten years. Borden presented his option of a Canadian navy and the prospect of Canada offering substantial financial assistance for Empire resources should a naval crisis materialise. Deep splits within his own party on the naval issue almost led to his being forced from the leadership, but he proved tenacious enough to see off the Conservative Party rebels. Outside the Province of Quebec, the rebels had been rather disorganised in their opposition to Borden.

The second great imperial issue of 1910 was trade reciprocity between Canada and the United States. Since the Liberal Government went for a very popular move (particularly among farmers in Western Canada) to eliminate customs duties on many agricultural and manufactured products, the best the Conservative Party could do was play the imperial card and claim it was an abandonment of Empire in favour of continentalism. Many businesses believed protectionism within the British Empire had served them well over the years, and the Conservatives launched a strong campaign against the trade arrangement, giving the electorate the choice of 'Canadianism or Continentalism'.[6] It was also the prospect of obtaining office that united the Conservatives throughout Canada. The 1911 general election was dominated by the issue of free trade, and business interests representing the railroads, banks, agriculture and manufacturing had a big say in the result. Canadian business fears of a Canada dominated by the economic interests of the United States meant that reciprocity was rejected.

While preparing to play golf at the Royal Ottawa Golf Club on 29 July 1911, Borden learnt the dramatic news that Parliament had been dissolved. The new 58-year-old Prime Minister in September 1911 was Robert Borden, with 133 Conservative seats to 86 Liberal seats and 2 Independents.[7] To Borden's further pleasure, the Conservative Party had won the majority of the popular vote. It was a great victory for the man who had united and structured an effective federal Conservative Party, a political party that still had strong provincial differences and could be seen as somewhat of a coalition of political interests. The two issues of free trade and the role for a Canadian navy had been prominent in Quebec, and the growth of French-Canadian nationalism was another product of the election. French-Canadian and anti-imperialist leaders like Henri Bourassa (known well to Borden since boarding together in Ottawa during Borden's first Parliament as a backbencher) did not like Borden's policies or the Conservatives, but they felt badly betrayed by Laurier. The Liberals still won more seats than the Conservatives in Quebec, but the growth of French-Canadian nationalism was evident and needed to be taken seriously by any national political party. The new Conservative Government set about introducing civil service reforms and trying to bring economic assistance to farmers.

In April 1912, Robert Borden also became the Secretary of State for External Relations alongside his position of Prime Minister. Not only did Robert Borden have the reliable Joseph Pope as his able Undersecretary of State for External Relations, but also Loring Christie as a personal adviser on

LORING CHRISTIE AND CANADIAN EXTERNAL AFFAIRS

Historians Robert Craig Brown, James Eayrs and Jack Granatstein have all singled out Loring Christie (1885–1941) for special consideration in determining Canadian external affairs. Eayrs is associated with the view that Christie was 'largely responsible for whatever intellectual coherence Canadian external policy possessed during the period 1918–1921'.[9] Norman Hillmer and Jack Granatstein describe his importance: 'Christie rapidly became the prime minister's key foreign policy counsellor, a source of facts, rationales and energy directed at gaining a potent role for Canada in the empire and globally.'[10] Christie was a brilliant lawyer who served Borden from 1913 until the end of his Administration and then also served Prime Minister Arthur Meighen. He did not have much sympathy with Meighen's successor, Prime Minister William Lyon Mackenzie King, who saw Christie as representing the previous Conservative (and Unionist) Administrations and their animosity ultimately led to Christie's resignation in May 1923.

foreign policy issues.[8] It was Loring Christie who had the task of directing Borden's wide-ranging ideas into more carefully produced policy statements.

The naval issue raised its head again in March 1912 as Borden moved away from Laurier's programme of constructing a Canadian navy while also complaining about not being merely an 'adjunct' to the British Empire.[11] Borden would propose a new naval programme by the end of the year, and the British First Lord of the Admiralty, Winston Churchill, presented a new construction programme for the Royal Navy. This largely derived from when Prime Minister Borden and a number of his colleagues (Honourable J D Hazen, Minister of Marine and Fisheries and Naval Service; Honourable L P Pelletier; Honourable C J Doherty and A E Blount, secretary) went to London to discuss a naval plan suitable for the Empire. Borden was pessimistic about the future state of Europe, and recounted in his memoirs: *During my visit to England in 1912, I had reached the conclusion that war was probably inevitable; but European conditions had seemed peaceful.*[12] He also took it upon himself to find out how the Imperial Defence Committee would function if war broke out. This allowed Borden to make similar organisational arrangements in Canada when he returned.[13]

A number of social gatherings were arranged, including Borden meeting David Lloyd George, then Chancellor of the Exchequer, but more significant work was undertaken with the First Lord of the Admiralty, Winston Churchill. Churchill, true to his disposition, did not pull his punches, and suggested to Borden that immediate support and relief were needed from Canada. This culminated in Canada's Naval Aid Bill – the planned development of three Dreadnoughts, costing some $35 million (Canadian dollars), to be at the disposal of the British for the defence of Empire in the event of war.[14] It was agreed that Canadian sailors would serve aboard these vessels. In turn, Borden felt he had won the concession from Britain that no significant foreign policy moves would be made in London without consulting a Canadian representative in advance. Prime Minister Herbert Asquith appeared to state as much in the British House of Commons: 'Side by side with this growing participation in the active burdens of the Empire on the part of the Dominions, there rests with us undoubtedly the duty of making such response as we can to their obviously reasonable appeal that they should be entitled to be heard in the determination of policy and the direction of Imperial affairs.'[15] Borden believed he had achieved a consultative role, but in reality this was not to take place.

During my visit to England in 1912, I had reached the conclusion that war was probably inevitable; but European conditions had seemed peaceful.

ROBERT BORDEN, *MEMOIRS*, 1938

Nevertheless, as long as he could give the reasonable impression that this had been achieved, he was in a good position domestically.

Sir Wilfrid Laurier saw the Naval Aid Bill, which included the $35 million for the defence of the British Empire, as an expedient rather than an emergency.[16] The Naval Aid Bill debate, which went on for a number of weeks, caused much anger and bitterness within the Canadian Parliament; the Bill did pass in the House of Commons on 15 May 1913, only to be rejected by the Senate in May 1914 in a vote of 51 to 27.[17] It was the long period of previous Liberal Governments which had allowed a large number of Liberals to be appointed to the House of Lords that helped to defeat the Bill. Canada would not deliver the emergency contribution to naval resources for Britain. Charles Stacey describes the failures over the Naval Bill as a 'national disaster'. He continues: 'There was no contribution to the Imperial fleet. At the same time, there was virtually no Canadian navy. The Naval Service Act of 1910 remained on the statute book, the two old cruisers that had been purchased remained in Canadian possession but were neglected and only partially manned; no new ships were built and no personnel recruited. When war broke out in 1914 Canada depended for the defence of her coasts upon British, Australian and Japanese ships'.[18] Canada's two warships, the *Rainbow* and the *Niobe* were much derided, inside and outside Canada, as being of little military significance.

Borden had been made a member of the Privy Council on his visit to England in 1912, and he was to become Sir Robert Borden in June 1914 (awarded the GCMG). He was the last Canadian Prime Minister to be knighted because in 1919 the Nickle Resolution (named after Canadian Conservative Member of Parliament, William Folger Nickle) prevented

Canadians obtaining peerages and knighthoods. Although the Resolution was passed by the Canadian House of Commons it was not an Act of Parliament and allowed Prime Minister Richard Bedford Bennett much later and briefly to reintroduce titles. Borden, despite being knighted, and in line with most Canadian Prime Ministers since, was in agreement with the Resolution: *They are very unpopular and entirely incompatible with our institutions.*[19] Borden, as will be seen, considered himself closer to the common man and found reason to rail against the aristocratic nature of the failed military leadership of the British during the First World War, and this might have influenced his views on honours.

Sir Robert Borden in London before the Peace Conference of 1919

II

The Paris Peace Conference

4

Rough Road to Versailles: the First World War and the Planning for Peace

War came in August 1914, and as in other parts of the British Empire, excited Canadian volunteers believed they might not get to Europe quickly enough to take part in hostilities; it was assumed the war would not last for very long. This miscalculation by politicians and the public had domestic and international ramifications for Canada, and the longevity and nature of the war clearly affected attitudes towards the eventual peace settlements.

Robert Borden and his wife cut short a golfing holiday in Muskoka, Ontario to be back in Ottawa on 1 August. Coming off the golf course, he was presented with a telegram from his ministers that urged his return. *We were in Council on August 4th at eleven and again at four. During the evening, while again in Council, at 8.55 p.m. the momentous telegram arrived announcing that war had been declared. Immediately, an Order-in-Council was passed summoning Parliament to meet on August 18th.*[1] In concluding his speech to the House of Commons on 18 August, Borden reminded his audience of their duty: *we stand shoulder to shoulder with Britain and the other British Dominions in this quarrel. And that duty we shall not fail to fulfil as the honour of Canada demands. Not for love of battle, not for lust of conquest, not for greed of possessions, but for the cause of honour, to maintain solemn pledges, to uphold principles of liberty, to withstand forces that would convert the world into an armed camp; yea, in the very name of the peace that we sought at any cost save that of dishonour, we have entered into this war; and while gravely conscious of the tremendous issues involved and of all the sacrifices that they may entail, we do not shrink from them, but with firm hearts we abide the event.*[2]

Borden saw the British Empire's cause as noble and moral, and emphasised the action now required on the part of Canada. It was clearly an almost religious occasion for him, and the serious tone was maintained by emphasising the sacrifices required by Canadians.[3] Anxieties were evident from the Government and opposition, but the general enthusiasm for the war by the public and parliamentarians was nevertheless evident; a general assumption prevailed that triumph would be fairly quickly delivered for the righteous cause.

Strangely, it was Sir Wilfrid Laurier as Leader of the Opposition who captured the history books with his eloquent speech to Parliament on 19 August. In approving of the Government's position, he further confirmed the nature of Anglo-Canadian relations. 'When the call comes, our answer goes at once, and it goes in the classical language of the British answer to the call to duty: "Ready, aye, ready".'[4] The problem with this widely supported approach was that this rush to arms to support Great Britain was prepared without creating any demands. The war was initially portrayed within and outside Canada as an obligation rather than a foreign policy opportunity. Even if long-term foreign policy planning was initially absent from Canadian thinking, the First World War and the resultant Paris Peace Conference produced a number of serious foreign policy opportunities for Canada.

Historian Robert MacGregor Dawson summarises the almost mundane constitutional situation for Canada at the outbreak of the war: 'The British declaration legally committed the whole Empire, although the Dominions had taken no part in the diplomacy which preceded the declaration, nor in the decision which irrevocably committed them to war.'[5] The Canadian decision was for their Government formally to inform Great Britain of their support and summon Parliament to determine the extent of their participation. No material demands had been made directly by Great Britain on Canada.

Sir Robert Borden tried to make it very clear within Cabinet and Parliament exactly what Canada's war aims were and how they should be expressed to the Canadian public. A lot of time was spent by the Government developing legal arguments as to why Canada should support Great Britain, and Loring Christie was directed by Robert Borden towards the published legal work of Lassa Oppenheim to find just cause as to why Canada should be involved in a war. It becomes a legalistic and self-justifying legal approach: 'At the heart of Borden's concept of Canadian war aims was the assumption that the law must be used as an instrument of war as the basic rationale for Canadian participation in the war.'[6]

Canadians were unprepared for the requirements that accompanied the advent of war in August 1914. However, the Canadian Government was quick to react to the necessities of being at war, even if it did not have the administrative infrastructure to cope with all the organisational burdens and may have appeared rather naive in what members believed could be achieved. Allocation of resources in wartime was more demanding than in peacetime, and new industrial and agricultural production levels had to be reached. The correct resources had to be marshalled into the appropriate areas for the war effort; not an easy task. Parliament passed a number of far-reaching war measures: The War Appropriations Act, The War Measures Act, The Finance Act, The Dominion Notes Act and The Customs Tariff Amendment Act. These included making financial provision to support the war, manufacturing goods for the war and recruiting the civilian population to provide front line troops. This at times made for an intolerable load for Robert Borden and made him mildly irritable with colleagues, but to his credit it was usually because he realised the seriousness of his work and the depth of the problems involved.

Sending troops to England was rather hastily ordered by Borden, and after an initial organisation and brief training at Valcartier Camp, near Quebec City, the more substantial training of the troops had to be delivered in England during winter. Canada was not involved in the strategic planning of the prosecution of the war. Borden, Brown notes, 'was not consulted about the strategy or the tactics adopted by the British High Command. He was not consulted about any significant aspect of the imperial government's war policy'.[7] This certainly remained the case until 1916. Borden famously told what was initially a small audience, *there will not be compulsion or conscription*, but the import of this reached a rather large audience, and Borden was not the first or last to regret a hasty pronouncement.

On 3 October 1914 a Canadian Expeditionary Force of 31,200 soldiers sailed for Plymouth, England, to be stationed for further training on a rather blustery Salisbury Plain. This training was insufficient against the use of artillery shells, machine guns and poison gas. 'In February 1915,' Kathleen Saunders points out, 'the first Canadians had reached Flanders. On April 22 at Ypres the Canadian troops held fast when the French colonial line broke against a devastating German chlorine gas attack. In three days the Canadians suffered 6,000 casualties.'[8] The casualty lists made for grim reading in Ottawa and throughout Canada as modern industrial warfare took its toll. The association with the war effort for most of the Canadian volunteers was Britain; half of them had been born in Britain and were only recent immigrants to Canada. Of this initial tranche of Canadian volunteers, the likelihood existed that many were primarily fighting for Great Britain and not necessarily Empire, or, for that matter, Canada.

This level of contribution from Canada was seemingly being made without any promises from the British Government for changes in Canada's status in international law. Yet Borden clearly felt that the efforts of Canadians should and would be rewarded with a greater say in the issues that determine war and peace.

One of Borden's more regretful decisions was to appoint Colonel Sam Hughes as the Minister of Militia and Defence. At first he stood out as at least one member of the Cabinet with military experience, and he did rather swiftly set up the Valcartier Camp. But Hughes had an ability to be rude and offensive, to overstep his military authority, and allegations of profiteering from war contracts pursued him. He was found by a Government commission to have been rather naive in some of his decisions to award contracts rather than having been involved in actual wrong-doing. Another of the training camps he organised – Camp Borden near Barrie, Ontario – was mismanaged to the extent that there was a riot there, which did Hughes little good as he headed for Europe in 1916 – and neither did the name of the camp do Borden any favours. In trying to reorganise Canadian forces in his own peculiar way in Europe and creating his own 'empire', Hughes went too far for even the tolerant Prime Minister, and he was sacked in a reorganisation from Ottawa. Nevertheless, one thing Borden was to have in common with Hughes was a critical stance on the British military's organisation of the war.

In secret travel arrangements, Borden, at the invitation of the British coalition government, sailed for England in June 1915 aboard the White Star liner *Adriatic*. With him was a future Prime Minister, Richard B Bennett, a very successful lawyer and member of parliament from Calgary who had rather good contacts in Britain (including the Canadian businessman, Max Aitken, who had relocated to London). *The Times* announced on 29 June that Borden would be visiting Great Britain, without specifying the date. The newspaper was aware of issues to come: 'The relations between the Mother Country and the Dominions can never be again as they were before the war, and wise and permanent adjustment of these relations depends greatly upon the Prime Minister of Canada.'[9] Not only did Borden want to be closer to decision-making concerned with the violent events in Europe, he also wanted some lucrative defence contracts for Canada. On the six-and-a-half week trip to England and France he visited wounded Canadian soldiers in 52 different hospitals.[10] On the political front he attended a British Cabinet meeting at the invitation of the British Prime Minister, Herbert Asquith. For all the cordiality of the meetings, Asquith was not granting decision-making powers to the Dominions over the prosecution of the war.

In England, a bold approach was initially evident from the Canadian Prime Minister as he argued the case for Canada being kept better informed about the war effort and sought more business contracts for additional supplies from Canada from David Lloyd George, the Minister of Munitions. War production from Canada subsequently increased dramatically, which is indicative of Borden's personal and political commitment to the war. Yet, in 1915 and 1916 there was no practical increase in the decision-making role of Canada in the First World War. To Andrew Bonar Law, the Colonial Secretary, Borden made it clear in a telegram that he wanted more information: *We thoroughly realise necessity central control of Empire armies but Governments of overseas Dominions have large responsibilities to their people for conduct of war, and we deem ourselves entitled to fuller information and to consultation respecting general policy in war operations.*[11]

Sir George Halsey Perley (1857–1938) held Canadian and American nationality and was a successful lumber merchant. He was elected as the Conservative Member of Parliament for Argenteuil, Quebec in 1904. For the period 1914–22 he was High Commissioner for Canada to the United Kingdom; this was initially considered only a temporary appointment from June 1914 to October 1917 and he is thus listed as Acting High Commissioner for his early time in London. For a year starting 31 October 1916 he was also to become Minister of Overseas Military Forces of Canada in the United Kingdom. His further public service included a brief period as Secretary of State for Canada in Arthur Meighen's Government in 1926 and as a Minister without Portfolio in Richard Bennett's Administration from 1930–5.

Sir George Halsey Perley conveyed the message to Bonar Law, who procrastinated in his reply, which further annoyed Borden. In 'private' Borden aired some of his frustrations, sending a further letter to Perley on 4 January 1916, which showed a high degree of his personal irritation with the British Government. *It can hardly be expected that we shall put 400,000 or 500,000 men in the field and willingly accept the position of having no more voice and receiving no more consideration than if we were toy automata. Any person cherishing such an expectation harbours an unfortunate and even dangerous delusion. Is this war being waged by the United Kingdom alone or is it a war waged by the whole Empire? If I am correct in supposing that the second hypothesis must be accepted, then why do the statesmen of the British Isles arrogate to themselves solely the methods by which it shall be carried out in the various spheres of warlike activity and the steps which shall be taken to assure victory and a lasting peace?*[12]

Borden made it clear in a separate telegram of 12 January (which arrived in London before the letter) that he did not want any action taken on the letter, so despite the strong image of Canada playing the role of automata, Borden still wished to be diplomatic. The original letter also had a very telling concluding paragraph: *Procrastination, indecision, inertia, doubt, hesitation and many other undesirable qualities have made themselves entirely too conspicuous in this war.*[13] The final sentence was equally damning: *Another very able Cabinet Minister spoke of the shortage of guns, rifles, munitions, etc., but declared that the chief shortage was of brains.*[14] Robert Craig Brown's analysis of the 'toy automata' letter suggests it was not a momentary lapse into bad temper: 'Rather it crystallized the accumulated grievances of Borden and his government over the whole range of inadequate consultation and co-operation since August 1914.'[15]

Procrastination, indecision, inertia, doubt, hesitation and many other undesirable qualities have made themselves entirely too conspicuous in this war.

ROBERT BORDEN, 4 JANUARY 1916

Borden's contacts made in Britain in 1915, the previous year, were not wasted, particularly since Lloyd George took over from Asquith as Prime Minister in December 1916. It was the honesty of Lloyd George over the impact that Great Britain could have on the war that worried Borden. He would ruminate on Lloyd George's words of August 1915, that *Great Britain would not be ready to exert full force for year or 18 months.*[16] Lloyd George, in his first speech to the House of Commons as Prime Minister, undertook to announce an Imperial Conference for 1917. Yet there was pragmatism in Lloyd George's interest in Borden; as one historian explains, 'Lloyd George encouraged Borden's involvement in a manner which was certainly deliberate but which was also probably unavoidable. The longer the war went on, the more important became the material assistance of Canada, which out of the Dominions had the most to offer – and the most to lose.'[17]

Back in Canada, during the evening of 13 February 1916, fire had engulfed the Parliament building in Ottawa. Borden had been ushered to safety but an MP, three Government employees and two visiting guests were killed. The unfounded notion of German sabotage heightened fears, and a large contingent of soldiers stood guard over the smouldering building where the House of Commons and Senate chambers had been destroyed. By the next afternoon the House of Commons was meeting in the Victoria Memorial Museum and Borden managed to instil an atmosphere of work as normal. Yet, of course things were not as normal and Borden got the approval of Laurier (and the British Parliament) to seek an amendment to the British North America Act of 1867 to extend the life of Parliament for a year and consequently delay any general election.

It was David Lloyd George's policy of creating an Imperial War Cabinet that opened the door for Canada to have a bigger say in the conduct of the First World War and the peace conference that would follow. In December 1916, the Prime Ministers of the Dominions and representatives of India were invited to London, ostensibly as equals in the decision-making process to be undertaken. A severe winter Atlantic crossing on the British armed mercantile cruiser *Calgarian* was how Borden travelled to England in February 1917. '*Calgarian* churned through the fog not daring to blow her horn or show her lights.' [18] If the difficulty of the journey might seem exaggerated, this ship was torpedoed by the Germans in March 1918 and sank with the loss of 49 lives.

David Lloyd George (1863–1945), lawyer and Liberal politician, was first elected to the British House of Commons in 1890. By 1905 he had become President of the Board of Trade and in 1908 the Chancellor of the Exchequer, and was considered a rather dynamic minister for his time. In 1916 he became Secretary of State for War and on 6 December of the same year, after the resignation of Herbert Asquith, he became Prime Minister. He has attracted polarised views about his political style and achievements; one strong view is that he adopted a presidential style of governance. As a dominant presence at the Paris Peace Conference, his personality and policies were a strong influence on the settlements. The foreign policy crisis in Chanak in Turkey contributed to his political downfall, and on 19 October 1922 he resigned as Prime Minister.

On arrival in England, the representatives of the Dominions and India had constitutional issues directed towards an Imperial War Conference. Lloyd George was making the strong point on behalf of the Dominions: 'They were fighting not for us but with us.' [19] Although this was opportunistic by Lloyd George, Britain needed the support of a lot more troops; it was equally opportunistic for Canada to press for constitutional considerations. Lloyd George created the Imperial War Cabinet to aid decision-making with the Dominions and between 20 March 1917 and 31 December 1918 it convened 48 times.[20]

A Conservative Member of Parliament, Leopold Amery, is sometimes given credit for the idea of establishing another body, the Imperial War Cabinet. Philip Wigley clarifies their roles: 'The Imperial War Cabinet, and a concurrent subsidiary Imperial War Conference, were therefore obliged to serve a multiple purpose; to register the dominions' claims as regards their constitutional and functional place in the empire; to brief their representatives on current problems; and finally, with due acknowledgement of dominion rights in any future scheme of things, to give overseas ministers a voice as to the possible terms of peace.'[21]

Sir Robert Borden in 1917 gave his full support to these two Cabinets (Imperial War Cabinet and Imperial War Conference) meeting in London, noting of the Imperial War Cabinet: *To its deliberations have been summoned representatives of all the Empire's self-governing Dominions. We meet there on terms of equality under the presidency of the First Minister of the United Kingdom; we meet there as equals, although Great Britain presides, primus inter pares.*[22]

In reality, there were three 'Cabinets' (British War Cabinet, the Imperial War Cabinet and the Imperial War Conference) operating in London at the same time. Some shared jurisdiction spilled over from one Cabinet group to another, but they appeared to function decidedly well. Prime Minister of Australia, William (Billy) Morris Hughes, was to later comment in his memoir of 1929 on the circumstances in 1917: 'For the first and only time in history one may truly say that the Empire was not governed from Downing Street.'[23]

When Borden arrived in London in February 1917 he had time on his hands, since the first Imperial War Cabinet did not take place until a month after his arrival, beginning 20 March. It allowed Borden time to become familiar with War

Cabinet documents which were supplied to him by British civil servants. 'Being privy to the innermost secrets of imperial war policy was almost like a dream come true for Borden and his colleagues, but the reality of being involved in policy-making under these circumstances was tough. It was an overwhelming experience, revealing the many sides, complexities, and contradictions of foreign and war policy which had seemed so simple and straightforward from the Ottawa perspective.' [24] The detailed discussions of the Imperial War Cabinet, taking place over fourteen meetings, related to military matters, finance and eventually the potential peace settlements.

Robert Borden made a good impression on Lloyd George when he argued against territorial expansion, as Lloyd George recounts in his own memoirs where he records the words of Borden on territorial growth: *if the chief result of this war was a scramble for territory by the Allied nations, it would be merely a prelude to further wars.*[25] The Canadian view was that the war was not being fought for the territorial expansion of the British Empire, and since Canada was the closest to the United States in political attitudes and development, Borden expressed the presumed opposition of the United States to any further attempts to expand the Empire. Borden ruminated on the difficulties President Woodrow Wilson faced because of Irish-Americans and German-Americans within the American nation. This was a strong argument for a mandate system to be covered by the League of Nations.

... if the chief result of this war was a scramble for territory by the Allied nations, it would be merely a prelude to further wars.

ROBERT BORDEN TO DAVID LLOYD GEORGE

Resolution IX

It was at the Imperial War Conference of 1917 that Borden presented a resolution which would eventually define the Commonwealth. Borden promoted *full recognition of the Dominions as autonomous nations of an Imperial Commonwealth* [26] It was Resolution IX, put forward by Borden and supported by the South African Minister of Defence, Jan Christian Smuts, which foreshadowed a declaration by Balfour in 1926 and the development of a British Commonwealth of Nations that was formally created in 1931 by the Statute of Westminster. From 1917, the term 'Commonwealth' was increasingly employed by representatives of the Dominions to describe their position with regards to the British Empire. The Dominions increasingly saw themselves as self-governing in foreign policy matters. Resolution IX elaborated on the matter that for the Dominions and India, there should be '... an adequate voice in foreign policy and in foreign relations, and ... effective arrangements for continuous consultation in all important matters of common imperial concern.' [27] It was a very bold claim for recognition, a recognition within the community constituting the British Empire and Dominions so that British Empire and Dominion unity was still intact.

Yet constitutional author Robert MacGregor Dawson highlights some of the ambiguities in Resolution IX in its vagueness of language. What was an 'adequate voice', 'full recognition', 'effective arrangements' or 'important matters'? These are hospitable phrases capable of satisfactory interpretation from a number of sides. Nevertheless, the Resolution should still be considered 'one of the landmarks in Empire history'.[28]

Borden had managed to head off those who believed

The founders of the academic political journal *The Round Table* in 1910 were Lord Milner, Geoffrey Dawson, Philip Kerr and in particular Lionel Curtis. The original subtitle of the journal was 'A Quarterly Review of the Politics of the British Empire'. Lionel Curtis (1872–1955) was editor of the journal from 1919–21, helped create the Royal Institute of International Affairs (Chatham House) in 1920, was a lecturer in colonial history at the University of Oxford and held a fellowship at All Souls College, Oxford. He was one of the disciples of Alfred Milner, Viscount Milner (1854–1925), High Commissioner in South Africa, who had assisted in the administrative rebuilding of South Africa after the Boer War. Lord Milner served in Lloyd George's War Cabinet as a minister without portfolio, was appointed Secretary of State for War in 1918 and head of the Colonial Office in December 1918. He was a member of the British delegation to the Paris Peace Conference that signed the Treaty of Versailles. Philip Henry Kerr, Marquess of Lothian (1882–1940) was editor of *The Round Table* 1910–17. Geoffrey Dawson (1874–1944) was Private Secretary to Lord Milner in South Africa, became the editor of *The Times* 1912–19 and 1932–41, and editor of *The Round Table* 1941–4.

imperialist development should follow a federalist approach. Lord Milner and a group associated with the journal *The Round Table* pursued the argument that imperial integration, based around federalism, was a good idea. Of those associated with *The Round Table*, Lionel Curtis was a particularly strong advocate of imperial federalism. However, Borden and Smuts were not imperial federalists and managed to prevail with their solution to imperial development somewhere between independence and federation.[29]

Conscription

If Borden was successful in constitutional issues relating to foreign policy that would have far-reaching consequences, the domestic issue of conscription also had long-lasting repercussions, reappearing again in controversial circumstances during the Second World War and affecting French-Canadian nationalism for a long time after. Borden appears to have very much made the decision in a belief that compulsory military service was important for the nation. The Canadian Expeditionary Force at Easter 1917 suffered 10,602 casualties at Vimy Ridge.[30] Although in 1917 the entry into the war by the United States (approved by Congress on 6 April 1917) appeared to alleviate manpower problems, the overthrow of the Tsar and exit of Russia from the war released enemy forces from the Eastern Front that could be deployed against the Allies on the Western Front.

On his return from Europe, Borden notified his Cabinet of the need for conscription in Canada, and on 18 May he went before Parliament to present his policy. The speech was emotive as he presented a *call from the wounded, the men in the trenches and those who have fallen* ... Borden was introducing *compulsory military enlistment on a selective basis [of] such reinforcements as may be necessary to maintain the Canadian army in the field as one of the finest fighting units of the Empire.*'[31] Getting the Military Service Bill passed by an emotional House of Commons and keeping Canada united were still tricky problems, and the Bill did not pass into law until 28 August. Anti-conscription views ran high in Quebec, where French-Canadians presented the war as imperial rivalry in which they had little interest, a stance that obtained some support among non-British immigrants in other parts of Canada. Borden, in turn, relied on the fact that many Liberals outside Quebec accepted conscription, dividing the Opposition Party but not necessarily the country. Wilfrid Laurier, at 76 years of age, could not hold the Liberal Party united against conscription and 22 Liberal Party members outside Quebec voted for conscription.

Alongside conscription, Borden created a coalition government in the hope of maintaining national unity. Borden stressed the necessity of unity among the political parties for the purpose of winning the war. Borden had been impressed with the coalition government created by Lloyd George in Britain, and he felt he could obtain the support of conscriptionist Liberals in Canada. The big fish to land, Laurier, would not join a coalition government, however, and made the creation of one more difficult. It took months of negotiation, but Borden devised a coalition in a new Unionist Government that managed to produce a Cabinet with eight Liberals. In two different approaches, Borden had developed the idea of unity with a Unionist Government in Canada, while undermining the structure of Canadian unity by introducing conscription.

In a move that blatantly reflected political skulduggery, the Wartime Elections Act was passed through Parliament on 20 September 1917. The summary of Robert Craig Brown is very succinct: 'It was a bald, reprehensible gerrymander, designed to ensure a conscriptionist vote and to eliminate anti-conscriptionist support in western Canada.'[32] In enfranchising female relatives of serving military personnel, the conscriptionist cause was advanced. The anti-conscriptionist cause was disadvantaged by denying the vote to those who had arrived in Canada from enemy countries over the previous years. Given that conscientious objectors were disenfranchised, the likelihood of the Government obtaining a further electoral mandate was quite high.

Borden put this new position to the electorate in a general election set for 17 December 1917, an election that proved to be explosive in a number of ways. During the campaign on 5 December, the Halifax disaster took place. A collision between a French munitions ship, the *Mont Blanc*, and a Belgian steamer, the *Imo*, caused the deaths of 1,630 people. The explosion, believed to be the largest man-made explosion in the world to that date, took place at the northern end of Halifax and demolished the naval dockyard, breweries, printing houses and warehouses. Fires destroyed many of the wooden buildings, including homes. Borden's sharp reaction in lending personal support at the scene and quickly arranging financial support gained him considerable credit. Nothing would swing the French-Canadian Liberals to his Unionist cause, but Borden was victorious in the general election. The result was a landslide victory for the Unionists (Conservatives and Unionist Liberals) with 153 seats in the House of Commons, compared to 82 seats for the Liberals led by Laurier. As predicted, the armed forces and their families supported the Unionists in large numbers.[33] The Conservative Party was split over the issue of the necessity of a Unionist Government and the Liberals were particularly divided over conscription, but somehow this situation had conspired to be to the electoral benefit of Borden.

After the election Borden could introduce domestic changes, including voting rights for women over 21. He also introduced in Canada a temporary prohibition on alcoholic beverages of more than 2.5 per cent alcohol – the prohibition was deemed to help improve the work rate of employees and also the grain could be used for essential food products.[34]

What had concerned Borden from fairly early on in the war was Britain's handling of the war or rather the mishandling of the war. An increasing worry for Borden was the longevity of the war and the inability of commanders to proffer an adequate strategy for the successful conclusion of the war or for an efficient supply of munitions. The strategies and leadership of the British High Command were seen by Borden as incompetent and class-ridden. This view persisted as the war dragged on, and Borden at a War Cabinet meeting in London on 13 June 1918 put forward his beliefs in the causes of battlefield failures: *it seems apparent, having regard to the material of which the British Army is composed, that the unfortunate results which have obtained during the past year, and especially during the past three months, are due to lack of foresight, lack of preparation, and to defects of system and organization.*[35]

Rather than weakening Borden's position with Lloyd George, his outburst at British officialdom strengthened their relationship. Borden was saying the very things that Lloyd George believed but was reluctant to air before his own supporters. Whether Lloyd George wanted to hear the criticism that Borden expressed in a private gathering over tea is another matter. *Mr Prime Minister, I want to tell you that, if ever there is a repetition of the battle of Passchendaele, not a Canadian soldier will leave the shores of Canada as long as the Canadian people entrust the government of their country to my hands.*[36]

Equally dramatic was Borden's expressions of frustration that the progress towards agreement on constitutional change for the Empire and the Dominions was taking a long time. Borden was happy that better communications existed during the Imperial War Cabinet meetings, although this was not as evident at other times, but he wanted more say for the Dominions in imperial foreign policy. Borden threatened on 23 July 1918: ... *unless [Canada] could have that voice in the foreign relations of the Empire as a whole, she would before long have an independent voice in her own foreign affairs outside the empire.*[37]

One of the prices to pay for Canadian involvement in decision-making in London was the need to travel. In May 1918, Borden went to England, and then again in November when German surrender looked to be plausible. Historians have emphasised the rather dry and uninformative nature of the dispatches that were sent from London to Ottawa.[38] This appears to have been partly because of the secrecy involved in the work being undertaken, and partly the style in which Borden communicated. It could also be argued that for all that Borden had won in theory about better communication between London and the Dominions, difficulties of having comprehensive and involved decision-making over serious crises on the battlefields of Europe was impractical.

Russian intervention

The impact of new responsibilities appeared to drive Canada into other areas of military involvement. Allied intervention in Russia fell into an area that could be seen as relevant to the war effort, since it was initially required to prevent supplies falling into the hands of the Germans. However, the broader policy appeared to be to oppose the Bolsheviks, but of course the likelihood of a Bolshevik-style revolution in Canada, even with trade union unrest, appeared far-fetched. Borden supported the cause of those fighting against the Bolsheviks in Russia, and that may have been enough to require Canada to send troops to Murmansk and then Archangel (both sent from Scotland in September 1918). This military commitment, ironically, had to be reinforced during new commitments to the peace process in 1919. Although the expedition in Siberia was unpopular in Canada and a surprise to many, including the Acting Prime Minister of Canada, Borden stuck to his promises to the British Government, and by December

1918 had 2,500 Canadian servicemen in Siberia, but would not keep them there beyond the spring.[39] Of the 4,000 Canadian soldiers that were in Siberia, none took part in any action there. Even the great anti-Bolshevik and British War and Air Secretary, Winston Churchill, could not, in May 1919, convince Borden to retain Canadian troops (16th Canadian Field Artillery Brigade) longer in Northern Russia.[40]

End of the War

Having received from Lloyd George a telegram that peace was pending, Borden replied the next day on 28 October: *The press and people of this country take it for granted that Canada will be represented at the Peace Conference. I appreciate possible difficulties as to representation of the Dominions but I hope you will keep in mind that certainly a very unfortunate impression would be created and possibly a dangerous feeling might be aroused if these difficulties are not overcome by some solution which will meet the national spirit of the Canadian people.*[41]

It was on board the *Mauritania* sailing for England that Prime Minister Borden learned of the German armistice signature on Monday, 11 November. The terms of the armistice as it related to Germany, Turkey, Bulgaria and Austria needed careful consideration, as did the issues relating to the demise of the Russian, German and Austro-Hungarian Empires. This meant the mood of rejoicing was tempered by the considerations of the monumental work ahead and of course the sacrifices that had been made to get to this point. In considered thoughts, Borden wrote in his diary: *The world has drifted from its old anchorage and no man can with certainty prophesy what the outcome will be.*[42]

On 14 November 1918, *The Times* printed the Canadian

casualties during the war as 211,358. They included: killed in action – 34, 877; died of wounds or disease – 15,45; wounded – 152,779; presumed dead or missing 8,245.[43] These figures would be revised upwards: 'Of the nearly 620,000 Canadians who had participated in the Canadian Expeditionary Force, 59,544 had died and nearly 173,000 were injured.'[44] These losses and commitment to the war effort allowed Borden to make what might retrospectively be seen as a functionalist argument, a type of argument evident towards the end of the Second World War. Representation for Canada at a post-war peace conference should be related to the contribution Canada had made during the First World War.

The Canadian historian and soldier of the Canadian Expeditionary Force that served overseas during the First World War, Frederic H Soward, argued that the proper context of Canada's new foreign policy was won on the battlefield. 'Had it not been for the gallant men who stood fast at Ypres, stormed Regina Trench, climbed the heights of Vimy Ridge, captured Passchendaele and entered Mons on November 11, 1918, Sir Robert's arguments would have carried far less weight. It was Canadian blood which purchased the title deeds to Canadian autonomy in foreign affairs.'[45] What Borden also won for Canada was better information from the British Government. With offices at 2 Whitehall Gardens, the Canadians found themselves close to political decision-making and able to influence Government ministers as they established their interests in industrial and agricultural issues.

The two men leading Canada and Great Britain into the peace were Sir Robert Borden and David Lloyd George. Borden's biographer, Brown, has not only captured the quintessential nature of Borden, but also the similarities and differences with Lloyd George. 'Both men were short and stocky and a trifle vain about their appearance. But in character they were opposite. Borden was as restrained as Lloyd George was explosive. Borden was loyal to his colleagues to a fault; Lloyd George used his and ruthlessly discarded them. Both men laboured painstakingly over drafts of their public speeches. Borden's were heavy with fact and precedent; Lloyd George's flowed from flourish to flourish, inspiring his audience to action. Colleagues and contemporaries thought Lloyd George cunning, devious, without principle, characteristics never ascribed to Borden. If Borden was the apostle of caution and common sense, Lloyd George was the exponent of daring opportunism and bold imagination.'[46] Hillmer and Granatstein add: 'Together, the plodding Canadian and the Welsh wizard made an impressive team, and they helped to usher in a new way of looking at the British Empire.'[47]

'If Borden was the apostle of caution and common sense, Lloyd George was the exponent of daring opportunism and bold imagination.'

ROBERT CRAIG BROWN, *WAR MEMOIRS*, VOL IV, 1934

5 Anglo-Canadian Relations at Versailles

Charles Stacey observed about the Canadian situation at the end of the First World War, 'A self-governing colony evolving into a nation under the impulsion of a world crisis is bound to leave loose ends.'[1] These loose ends were taken into the Versailles Peace Conference.

Canada's claims for involvement in the peace process were dealt an early blow when President Woodrow Wilson's Fourteen Points were accepted in a pre-armistice agreement as a basis of the peace, but the Dominions were not consulted. The British Government, acting as the Imperial Government, accepted the Fourteen Points with some legal reservations. Although objections to the proposals by the Dominions would have been premature, the lack of consultation produced some disharmony between them and Britain. It was an awkward introduction for the Fourteen Points which constituted the basis of the Peace.

While at Claridge's Hotel in London in December 1918, Borden was reminded in a memorandum from the Acting Prime Minister of Canada, Sir Thomas White, of the

PRESIDENT WILSON'S FOURTEEN POINTS, 8 JANUARY 1918

The program of the world's peace, therefore, is our program; and that program, the only possible program, as we see it, is this:

I. Open covenants of peace, openly arrived at, after which there shall be no private international understandings of any kind but diplomacy shall proceed always frankly and in the public view.

II. Absolute freedom of navigation upon the seas, outside territorial waters, alike in peace and in war, except as the seas may be closed in whole or in part by international action for the enforcement of international covenants.

III. The removal, so far as possible, of all economic barriers and the establishment of an equality of trade conditions among all the nations consenting to the peace and associating themselves for its maintenance.

IV. Adequate guarantees given and taken that national armaments will be reduced to the lowest point consistent with domestic safety.

V. A free, open-minded, and absolutely impartial adjustment of all colonial claims, based upon a strict observance of the principle that in determining all such questions of sovereignty the interests of the populations concerned must have equal weight with the equitable claims of the government whose title is to be determined.

VI. The evacuation of all Russian territory and such a settlement of all questions affecting Russia as will secure the best and freest cooperation of the other nations of the world in obtaining for her an unhampered and unembarrassed opportunity for the independent determination of her own political development and national policy and assure her of a sincere welcome into the society of free nations under institutions of her own choosing; and, more than a welcome, assistance also of every kind that she may need and may herself desire. The treatment accorded Russia by her sister nations in the months to come will be the acid test of their good will, of their comprehension of her needs as distinguished from their own interests, and of their intelligent and unselfish sympathy.

VII. Belgium, the whole world will agree, must be evacuated and restored, without any attempt to limit the sovereignty which she enjoys in common with all other free nations. No other single act will serve as this will serve to restore confidence among the nations in the laws which they

have themselves set and determined for the government of their relations with one another. Without this healing act the whole structure and validity of international law is forever impaired.

VIII. All French territory should be freed and the invaded portions restored, and the wrong done to France by Prussia in 1871 in the matter of Alsace-Lorraine, which has unsettled the peace of the world for nearly fifty years, should be righted, in order that peace may once more be made secure in the interest of all.

IX. A readjustment of the frontiers of Italy should be effected along clearly recognizable lines of nationality.

X. The peoples of Austria-Hungary, whose place among the nations we wish to see safeguarded and assured, should be accorded the freest opportunity to autonomous development.

XI. Rumania, Serbia, and Montenegro should be evacuated; occupied territories restored; Serbia accorded free and secure access to the sea; and the relations of the several Balkan states to one another determined by friendly counsel along historically established lines of allegiance and nationality; and international guarantees of the political and economic independence and territorial integrity of the several Balkan states should be entered into.

XII. The Turkish portion of the present Ottoman Empire should be assured a secure sovereignty, but the other nationalities which are now under Turkish rule should be assured an undoubted security of life and an absolutely unmolested opportunity of autonomous development, and the Dardanelles should be permanently opened as a free passage to the ships and commerce of all nations under international guarantees.

XIII. An independent Polish state should be erected which should include the territories inhabited by indisputably Polish populations, which should be assured a free and secure access to the sea, and whose political and economic independence and territorial integrity should be guaranteed by international covenant.

XIV. A general association of nations must be formed under specific covenants for the purpose of affording mutual guarantees of political independence and territorial integrity to great and small states alike.

expectation of the Cabinet and the position of Canada within what was being described as the British Commonwealth. Resolution IX delivered at the Imperial War Conference of 1917 gave the expectation that constitutional change would be delivered. White wrote: 'Canada is of opinion that in view of war efforts of Dominions other nations entitled to representation at Conference should recognize unique character of British Commonwealth composed of group of free nations under one sovereign and that provision should be made for special representative of these nations at Conference even though it may be necessary that in any final decisions reached they should speak with one voice; that if this is not possible then you should form one of whatever delegation represents a British Commonwealth.'[2]

'A self-governing colony evolving into a nation under the impulsion of a world crisis is bound to leave loose ends.'
HISTORIAN CHARLES STACEY, *CANADA AND THE AGE OF CONFLICT*, 1977

Borden's thoughts were that *in the end, and perhaps sooner than later, Canada must assume full sovereignty.*[3] Canada had arrived in Europe not only concerned with the settlements but to confirm the foundation on which its formal participation would take place and in many ways to determine the shape of post-war imperial diplomacy. Both Borden and White were aware that the Canadian public should be kept informed of events in London and Paris and the Canadian delegation took with them one of Canada's most respected journalists, J W Dafoe of the *Winnipeg Free Press*. This was not to stop other Canadian publications following events; the inclusion of a sympathetic journalist merely served as a good public information exercise, and he was good company.

Besides the issue of representation, on 7 December 1918

White reminded Borden of Canada's reparation claims which were elevated to include not only war expenditure, but the costs of interruption to trade, damages for casualties and damages for the Halifax disaster, rather seriously put at $30 million.[4] White continued to press this claim to Borden, including repeating it in March 1919.[5] Claims for the Halifax disaster – the collision between a Belgian relief ship and a French munitions ship in Halifax harbour in 1917 – were not pursued as a reparations issue by Borden; the open door for lots of peripheral claims from states was wisely avoided.[6] He replied to White: *If we put forward Halifax claims as suggested it would strengthen French demand that their extraordinary reparation claims shall have complete precedence.*[7] There was a wide awareness that Germany would not be able to pay the reparation claims being asked for in early 1919, particularly the level and type of claims from France and Italy. The latter put in claims including cost of living increases since the end of hostilities.

In fact, Borden could largely ignore advice from Canada and considered himself as speaking for Canada as and when he desired. He would have one eye on any domestic political fallout from his decisions, but there was not a precedent for how he should behave at this international conference. The *Montreal Star* incorrectly presented Borden's position on reparations as being against the principle of indemnity. In fact, Borden wanted as much as Germany was capable of paying; it just was not clear what that financial amount was.

At the Imperial War Cabinet in December 1918 (its 48th meeting), alongside Billy Hughes, Prime Minister of Australia, Borden pressed for a strong representation for the Dominions at the Paris Peace Conference, although Canada did not expect as large a representation as France and Great

Britain. Hughes complained that the Dominions, under French proposals, appeared to be given representation similar to Sweden, and Borden protested that: *It would be regarded as intolerable in Canada that Portugal should have a representation in the Peace Conference which was denied to that Dominion. Canada had lost more men killed in France than Portugal had put in the field.*[8] The Imperial War Cabinet thus proposed, 'Representatives of the British Dominions and India ought to be present at the opening session and at any other session of the Peace Conference or the Allied Preliminary Conference (should it be held) at which Belgium and other smaller Allied States were represented ... The British Dominions and India should in all respects have the same powers as, and be on an equal footing at the conference with, Belgium and other smaller Allied States ... The Prime Ministers of the Dominions and the representatives of India should be placed on a panel from which part of the personnel of the British delegation could be filled, according to the subject for discussion.'[9]

The notion of a panel was confusing and appeared to mean that one of the five British delegates would be from the Dominions, chosen in turn from a panel. A French proposal confused matters further by not mentioning the Dominions. Both the Prime Ministers of Canada and Australia held out for representation being established individually and via the British Empire delegation. Representation for Canada was more important for Canada than any material benefits that might derive from representation; Canada was making no claim to additional territory. It is from this Imperial War Cabinet meeting, incorporating a speech by Borden, that the concept of the British Empire delegation derived (essentially the Imperial War Cabinet by a different name).[10] The upshot

Lord Robert Cecil (1864–1958), whose full name was Edgar Algernon Robert Gascoyne-Cecil, was elected as a Conservative to the British House of Commons in 1906, but was a rather independent Conservative. He served from 1915 to 1919 as Parliamentary Under-Secretary of State in the Governments of Herbert Asquith and David Lloyd George and also from February 1916 to July 1918 as the Minister of Blockade. Cecil's true passion became the League of Nations and he attended the Paris Peace Conference as a British delegate. Interestingly, Cecil represented South Africa at the early meetings of the League of Nations, 1920–22, and spent much of the rest of his life as an advocate of voluntary organisations, the League of Nations Union and by 1936 also the International Peace Campaign. He was Lord Privy Seal and Chancellor of the Duchy of Lancaster in the Governments of Stanley Baldwin in the 1920s, but it was his work as President of the British League of Nations Union 1923–45, to which he devoted much of his time. It was Cecil who under the League of Nations Union organised the Peace Ballot of 1934–5 in Britain, a national ballot that showed considerable public support for the League of Nations and the application of military sanctions. He was awarded the Nobel Peace Prize in 1937.

of this view was put in a telegram by Lord Robert Cecil and dispatched to Paris saying that the Dominions and India achieved a form of dual representation 'separately, as powers in their own right; and collectively as members of a British Empire delegation'.[11] Lloyd George had to sell this position to the other Allied delegates at Paris.

On 6 January 1919, the Acting Prime Minister in Ottawa again put pressure on Borden: 'Canadian people would not appreciate five American delegates throughout whole Conference and no Canadian entitled to sit throughout Conference nor would they appreciate several representatives from Great Britain and Canada none.'[12]

The Paris Peace Conference, despite delegations being in Paris for longer periods, ran from January 1919 through the signing of the Treaty of Versailles in June 1919 to January

SIR GEORGE EULAS FOSTER, CHARLES JOSEPH DOHERTY, AND ARTHUR LEWIS SIFTON

Sir George Eulas Foster (1847–1931) was born and educated in New Brunswick, Canada. As a Conservative and Unionist Member of Parliament he represented constituencies in New Brunswick and Ontario from 1882 to 1921. His Cabinet portfolios were as Minister of Marine and Fisheries, Minister of Finance and Receiver General, and Minister of Trade and Commerce. Foster had a reputation for being rather serious, and he was a campaigner for the prohibition of alcohol. The latter position he shared with his first wife, Addie Davies Chisholm, who was a founder of the Woman's Christian Temperance Movement of Ontario. Not only did Foster become a Canadian delegate to the Paris Peace Conference, he served on a number of Inter-Allied Committees there: Inter-Allied Economic Commission, Supreme Economic Council (British Empire Panel), British Empire Committee on Transport and Transit, and the British Empire Economic Committee. Foster also represented Canada at the first Assembly of the League of Nations and again in 1926 and 1929; and he delivered public lectures on the importance of the League of Nations.

Charles Joseph Doherty (1855–1931) was the Conservative and Unionist Member of Parliament for the constituency of St Anne, Quebec, 1908–21. He served as the Minister of Justice and Attorney General of Canada in the administrations of Robert Borden and Arthur Meighen. At the Paris Peace Conference, Doherty's specialized committee work was serving on the Supreme Economic Council, the Inter-Allied Sub-Committee on Pre-War Contracts and the British Empire Committee on the League of Nations. Further, Doherty became a Canadian delegate to the League of Nations, 1920–22.

Arthur Lewis Sifton (1858–1921) was the Unionist Member of Parliament for Medicine Hat, Alberta from 1917 to 1921. In this one period of an elected Government he was Minister of Customs, Minister of Inland Revenue, Minister of Customs and Inland Revenue, Minister of Public Works and Secretary of State for Canada. Previously he had been Premier of Alberta, 1910–17, and the first Chief Justice of the newly created province in 1905. Sifton supported Robert Borden in both the introduction of conscription and the formation of a Unionist Government.

Alongside Charles Doherty, Sifton signed the Treaty of Versailles for Canada, but his major accomplishments at the Paris Peace Conference were in regard to transportation, serving on the Inter-Allied Commission on the International Regime of Ports, Waterways and Railways; Inter-Allied Sub-Committee on the Regime of Rivers, Ports and Railways; Supreme Economic Council; and the British Empire Committee on Transport and Transit. Sifton also contributed to the discussions that created the conventions of the International Labour Organisation.

1920. The British Empire delegation, first meeting on 13 January, was made up of Great Britain, India and the Dominions (Australia, Canada, Newfoundland and South Africa) and these were effectively represented by plenipotentiary delegates (persons invested with full power to transact business). Canada had four delegates of this status: Sir Robert Laird Borden, Prime Minister; Sir George Eulas Foster, Minister of Trade and Commerce; Charles Joseph Doherty, Minister of Justice; and Arthur Lewis Sifton, Minister of Customs and Inland Revenue.[13]

On 11 January 1919, Robert Borden and his staff left London for Paris. The large number of international delegates descending on Paris made the allocation of suitable accommodation quite an issue.[14] The Canadian delegation had approximately 15 delegates and experts, but Serbia sent over 100. Loring Christie, who had been part of an advanced Canadian guard sent to Paris, reported to Borden that the office accommodation was in some confusion. On the journey to Paris, Lloyd George kept company with Borden for some of the trip. Despite the worries about available rooms in Paris, Borden was lodged in the sizeable Hotel Majestic, a hotel largely taken over by the British. Canadian administrative staff also worked out of the Hotel La Perouse, where a number of Canadian memoranda were produced from meetings that began at 10.30 am each day. The French staff had been replaced with British staff because of worries about information security. The downside for Borden was that it meant there were rather heavy English meals served every day and so he absented himself from a number of evening meals. Despite the complaints that would surface about the time that had to be spent in Paris, Borden's early impressions of being in the city were favourable. *Weather delightful,* he noted in his diary on 19 January, *somewhat cooler than it was last week. Paris more and more impresses me as a very beautiful city. London is far inferior in the artistic skill displayed in laying out modern streets.*[15]

Borden was restless at the Peace Conference, writing to Lloyd George that the *delays in advancing the business of the Peace Conference are unjustifiable and unnecessary.*[16] A week was devoted to procedures that Borden thought could be completed in less than two days. A number of Canadian representatives had been away from Ottawa since 8 November 1918 and, in January 1919, Borden complained on their behalf. He further complained that he had been in Paris for ten days and only one meeting (rather formal) of the full conference had been held. George Foster recommended modifying one of the letters because his complaints seemed to be rather strongly worded.[17]

Lloyd George was partly responsible for improving Robert Borden's general outlook whilst in Paris. Borden's opinions do appear to have been well-received by Lloyd George, but he was also capable of making Borden appear important. The British Prime Minister realised that his charm was one of his best weapons in getting what he wanted. Borden attended some private breakfasts and lunches with Lloyd George where he was informed of the major decisions taken by the leaders of the Big Five Powers (United States, France, Great Britain, Italy and Japan).[18] An example of the sort of information fed to Borden is a diary entry by him on 21 January, that reads: *Lloyd George thinks French are marking time so as to delay important questions until after President Wilson's departure.*[19]

Borden wisely managed to take French lessons in Paris; the lessons were provided by a Mademoiselle Perret, a tutor recommended by Colonel Oliver Mowart Biggar (Adviser on Military Questions of the Canadian delegation at the Peace Conference). As a consequence he made an increasing number of entries in his diary in French. The other diversion, if it was a diversion, was to sit for his portrait to be painted by Sir William Orpen, and he further visited the studio of Augustus John to have a portrait painted. From Borden's accounts of life in Paris, the Canadians appeared to partake of few frivolities. One evening after going to see *Cyrano de Bergerac* at the theatre and supper afterwards in the presence of the leading lady, Borden recounts, *This was one of the friskiest evenings of Foster's* [Sir George Foster] *life, as we kept him up until 1.15. I told him I never would have embarked on such an adventure without his presence as chaperon.*[20] This was a joke for Foster's colleagues, since they knew him as a total abstainer of alcohol and decidedly solemn in demeanour.

On Sunday 12 January 1919, the five Great Powers met (known as the Council of Ten due to the representatives including the Prime Ministers or first delegates and their Foreign Secretaries) and discussed the broader representation at the conference, with strong opposition voiced by the United States about the British Dominions. President Woodrow Wilson's objection was in part that *'if Canada and the other Dominions had the same representation as Belgium and the other small Allied nations they would stand in a much better position than Belgium as they would be backed by the British Delegation.'*[21]

It was reported to the first meeting of the British Empire delegation (apparently from information supplied by Lloyd George) that American Secretary of State Robert Lansing was 'arrogant not to say offensive,' questioning the right of Canada to be concerned in the settlement of European affairs.[22] Perhaps in a slightly obvious response, Lloyd George was to come to the defence of Canada, which was appreciated by Borden. Lloyd George's repost was twofold: '…they [Canada] believed themselves to have that right because some hundreds of thousands from the Dominions had died for the vindication of public right in Europe and that Canada as well as Australia had lost more men than the United States in this war.'[23] It could further and rather evidently be added that the United States is just as geographically removed from Europe as Canada.

It was begrudgingly agreed by the Council of Ten that two Canadian delegates could sit on the plenary sessions of the Peace Conference. Australia, South Africa and India also had two delegates and New Zealand to its disappointment one. Newfoundland had no delegate, but provided a representative for the British Empire delegation. Much of this was window-dressing and more concerned with recognition than a significant decision-making role. As is widely recorded, the five Great Powers and eventually Lloyd George, British Prime Minister; Georges Clemenceau, President of the Council of Ministers of France and President of the Peace Conference, and Woodrow Wilson, President of the United States, were the significant decision-makers. Philip Wigley posits in his historical work that the Dominions 'succeeded only in arming themselves for the wrong battle … because the important decisions … were taking place on ground hardly accessible to the Dominion ministers.'[24] As French President Clemenceau astutely observed, 'Sir Robert Borden has reproached us, though in a very friendly way … With your permission I will remind you [Borden] that it was we [the major Powers] who decided there should be a conference in Paris, and that the representatives of the countries interested should be summoned to attend it. I make no mystery of it – there is a Conference of the Great Powers going on in the next room.'[25]

Work of the Commissions

Although the real authority lay with the Supreme Council of the Allies, a lot of work was still carried out by committees and sub-committees and Sir Robert Borden had a long parliamentary career involved in committee work. Borden was a Vice-President on the Commission dealing with the problems affecting Greece, on the Inter-Allied Commission on the Russian Question and also prominent in dealing with the future of German colonies. He was also happy to represent Britain at a suggested conference with the Bolsheviks and Russian factions at Prinkipo, in the Sea of Marmara, but this did not take place.[26] The task of dealing with Greek and Turkish territorial claims proved to be a major challenge. The technical nature of many committees led Assistant Under-Secretary at the Foreign Office Sir Eyre Crowe (Minister Plenipotentiary at the Peace Conference) to criticise those playing a part who were not professional diplomats. '… Sir R Borden became the British 'expert' on Albania, Epirus, Thrace, Smyrna, etc., and Sir T Cook the expert on Czecho-Slovakia! The result was ludicrous and embarrassing.'[27]

Interestingly, Borden himself had strong views on the Italian and United States delegations on the Greek Committee, finding the Italians obstructionist from early stages and the United States lacking experience: *The American delegates are university men who depend wholly upon books, statistics and reports of missionaries. They are men of ability and of fine character and ideals; but their utter inacquaintance with public affairs and their outlook upon political conditions do not render them specially useful when difficult questions involving race, language, tradition, political association and future economic development have to be taken into account.*[28] Borden could indicate that there was concurrence from the major powers on the policies he pursued. All four powers (United Kingdom, United States, France and Italy) showed considerable agreement on the arrangements for Western and Eastern Thrace.

The British Empire delegation did consistently have formal meetings, getting together some 35 times between January and June 1919. Borden pressed Lloyd George to recognise Canada as a representative on the Committee considering establishment of the League of Nations. However, Lloyd George had a problem: why ask for Canada's representation without asking for representation for all of the other Dominions? He was honest about this dilemma and further felt he would have to consult the 'Lesser Powers' as well as the Great Powers on this. Philip H Kerr, Marquess of Lothian, Lloyd George's secretary, responded to Borden: 'He [Lloyd George] thinks the Dominions and the Empire have been very generously treated by the other nations of the world in the matter of representation, and that if we were to put forward further claims to representation, both as individual nations and as part of the British Empire, it might arouse the not unreasonable criticism and opposition of the other powers. He thinks that to raise such opposition now might seriously prejudice the question of the representation of the nations of the British Empire in the constitution of the League of Nations which is now under consideration, and where wealth and population rather than war service may be the principal considerations.'[29]

Lloyd George felt that General Smuts (Plenipotentiary of

South Africa at the Peace Conference) and Lord Robert Cecil (Adviser on the question of the League of Nations for the British delegation at the Peace Conference) had consulted with representatives of the Dominions in preparing drafts for the Commission. The situation remained that no Canadian sat on the Committee that drafted the Covenant of the League of Nations.[30]

Labour issues

An area Robert Borden wanted to make his own, but that makes him seem less creditable today, was international labour, or rather, responding to the report of the Commission on International Labour Legislation. Clearly, he felt labour issues could be very different in Canada to those of the United Kingdom and the British representatives would have an *imperfect knowledge* of this.[31] The International Labour Commission wanted to provide for an equality of treatment between foreign workers and nationals. Clause 8 for insertion in the Versailles treaty read: 'In all matters concerning their status as workers and social insurance foreign workmen lawfully admitted to any country and their families should be ensured the same treatment as the nationals of that country.'[32] Borden, mindful of the prejudice at home against Asian labour, warned of *great disorder, possibly rebellion on the Pacific Coast of the United States and of Canada.*[33] It also seemed appropriate for Borden to cite provincial differences within Canada on labour legislation, particularly British Columbia and Saskatchewan. However, the example of British Columbia he employed with Lloyd George was not entirely attractive. … *in British Columbia there is Provincial legislation which reserves certain industries for white labour. Apparently the eighth article of the proposed report would call upon us to override this legislation. Any such proposal would arouse the fiercest resentment and might lead to the most serious consequences.*[34] Lloyd George promised to hold a meeting of the British Empire delegation as soon as possible, but he clearly implied he had more important matters to deal with: 'I have been anxious to hold a Delegation meeting for the last ten days, but I have been meeting President Wilson, M Clemenceau and Signor Orlando morning and afternoon during this time because I felt that the one imperative thing was to force through an agreement in regard to the peace with Germany with the least possible delay.'[35] This rather unceremoniously put Canada more generally in its place, and not at the 'high table' of Conference decision-making.

The eventual clause was changed in Canada's favour, and read: 'The standard set by law in each country with respect to the conditions of labour should have due regard to the equitable economic treatment of all workers lawfully resident therein.'[36]

The International Labour Organisation also threw up the issue of membership, particularly with regard to its governing body. References to the word 'state' rather than 'member' put the self-governing Dominions in an awkward position, and they had to get drafts changed so they were not excluded from important positions. Henry Mauris Robinson, United States delegation adviser on labour and shipping questions at the Peace Conference, kicked up a fuss that through the Dominions, Great Britain was having a greater representation than it should, as if Canada were not going to be making independent judgements. Borden's feeling was that not only was the position of the United States inaccurate, but the United States had ignored its own influence on states like Cuba, Haiti, Panama, Salvador, Venezuela, Colombia and Liberia.

Canadian labour opinion is captured in a memorandum from Canadian representative to the Peace Conference Arthur Lewis Sifton to Borden. Again, Canadian workers are evoked, but this time as a group that would not accept humiliation on this point of representation. 'I rather anticipate that disregarding some views of theology they will say in their somewhat frank manner that they will see the Japanese and Italian delegates and their respective governments individually and collectively sizzling in the lowest depths of Hell before they will agree to accept a standing inferior to the negroes of Liberia.'[37]

Borden went further to suggest that the Canadian Parliament would not accept the humiliation of being excluded from the governing body of the League of Nations and might choose to withdraw from the League of Nations and the Labour Convention. *I am confident that the people of Canada will not tamely submit to a dictation which declares that Liberia or Cuba, Panama or Hedjaz, Haiti or Ecuador must have a higher place in the international labour organization than can be accorded to their country which is probably the seventh industrial nation of the world, if Germany is excluded from consideration.*[38]

The 'Inequality' clause

The Canadians in Paris were equally mindful of the Pacific Coast of Canada when the Japanese put forward a racial equality clause as part of the preamble of the Covenant of the League. The resolution appeared innocuous enough: 'By the endorsement of the principle of equality of all nationals of states members of the League.'[39] Lord Robert Cecil, British Empire delegation adviser on the question of the League of Nations at the Peace Conference, described the situation to

Borden as 'the very tiresome question of the Japanese'.[40] Cecil managed to get Borden to offer his diplomatic assistance in the matter. Borden did not particularly wish to upset the Japanese delegation or even more particularly domestic opinion in Canada that was wary of Asian immigration. Robert Borden suggested new wording, *By the endorsement of the principle of equality between nations and just treatment of their nationals*,[41] but this came to nothing (and neither did the suggestions of General Smuts and Lord Robert Cecil). This emphasis on *equality between nations*, of course, gave the resolution an entirely different meaning and was unacceptable to the Japanese. Given that public opinion in Japan was very interested in these developments, Japanese resentment towards the Western powers as a result of the rejected clause was not to be assuaged, but they did not refuse to join the League of Nations.

The British Empire delegation

Writing from the Hotel Majestic in Paris on 16 April 1919, Borden summarised for Lloyd George the events at the Council of Five the previous day. Borden had represented the British Empire delegation at a Council of Five meeting that lasted two hours. In a preface to his summary, Borden referred to Mr Lansing as being *afflicted with his usual tendency to defer and refer, hence the progress made was not so great as anticipated*.[42]

The surprisingly general areas discussed were: troops in occupied German territories, the convention on opium, Belgian treaties, the British Protectorate over Egypt, issues relating to Morocco, poison gases and German Prize Courts (national courts or tribunals that dealt with the enforcement of the principles of international law, in particularly the capture of naval forces of belligerent states). The cost of maintaining troops in German territories was passed to the Council of Four. Both the issues of Egypt and Morocco and Germany's renunciation of territorial interests were pushed by Lansing as issues that could be dealt with in a general clause, but this was left in abeyance. Lansing was also opposed to the Allied governments controlling all chemical processes in Germany that were employed to produce poison gases. The Prime Minister of Canada wrote: *The British proposal seems very comprehensive and would, if effectively carried out, result in the disclosure of German commercial secrets. I argued that if such secrets were employed for the destruction of human life by barbarous means during the war, Germany could not complain if their disclosure was compelled.*[43]

Again, Borden deferred this issue to the Council of Four. Lansing's proposal that the Allied and Associated Powers examine the decisions of the German Prize Courts was seen as impractical by Borden, and he hoped the Drafting Committee would develop principles on which to continue.

Trade

The Paris Conference also presented opportunities for Canada; these included the promotion of trade, and in particular trading opportunities with Balkan countries. Canada believed that international trade, controlled during the First World War, should be liberalised. Mr Lloyd Harris, adviser on financial, economic and labour questions for the Canadian delegation in Paris, was given the opportunity to communicate with the Serbian, Romanian and Greek governments. *It is his strong opinion that they offer remarkable opportunities for export trade in manufactured articles if satisfactory arrangements can be made to secure repayment within a reasonable period and to provide the necessary finances in the meantime. The climate of Roumania and Serbia is more like our own than is that of France and Belgium and the requirements of the people in manufactured articles are of a character that Canada can satisfy along lines of present production.*[44]

More generally, Canada wanted to see a secure international economy with stable exchange rates and responsible financial policies prevailing. Sir George Foster and Charles Doherty managed to organise trade credit for the French, so France could purchase Canadian products. This was done through the Canadian Trade Commission.

The League of Nations and Article X

The Canadian delegation at the Peace Conference became concerned as to whether or not they would be eligible for election to the Council of the League of Nations. The particular worry was that representatives of the Dominions would not be selected as members of the Council because they were not considered states. On behalf of Borden, Lloyd George obtained commitments from Wilson and Clemenceau that corroborated the right of the Dominions to be elected to the League of Nations Council. Borden obtained the signatures of all three on a memorandum he had prepared,[45] giving their agreement that 'the question having been raised as to the meaning of Article IV of the League of Nations Covenant, we have been requested by Sir Robert Borden to state whether we concur in this view that … *representatives of the self-governing Dominions of the British Empire may be selected or named as members of the Council*. We have no hesitation in expressing our entire concurrence in this view.'[46]

The main concern of the delegation was Article X of the Covenant of the League of Nations. This was no small matter, since the article was at the heart of the League of Nations' collective security system. It read: 'The Members of the League undertake to respect and preserve as against external aggression the territorial integrity and existing political independence of all Members of the League. In case of any such aggression or in case of any threat or danger of such aggression the council shall advise upon the means by which this obligation shall be fulfilled.'[47]

The problem for Canada was that this seemed too all-encompassing for a country that was a long way away from the potential trouble spots and unlikely to be directly invaded. Canadian Minister of Justice Charles J Doherty commented on the draft Covenant, and in particular, Article X, in a memorandum to Borden and colleagues sent on 22 February 1919: 'Of the gravity of the obligations by it imposed upon the parties to the Convention, there can be no question. It makes of the League, as *The Times* expresses it, "a mutual guarantee society of unlimited Liability".' Doherty continued by clearly questioning the wisdom of member states of the League 'undertaking in all the horrors of wars in which they had no interest, in order to ensure respect for decisions in which they had no part and for which they had no responsibility'.[48] He was also to say of Article X, that it was 'a mutual guarantee where the risks run and the burdens imposed are not equal between the nations entering into it, and where the inequality is particularly striking in the case of countries in Canada's position, and works specially to their detriment'.[49]

At the Hotel La Perouse on 13 March the Canadians prepared a memorandum dealing with their objections to articles of the Covenant of the League of Nations.[50] It was prepared for the British Empire delegation but also sent under a polite covering note to President Woodrow Wilson. In many areas, the memorandum just dealt with the omission of what they believed were unnecessary words. The Canadian delegation made for better solicitors than even the British delegation. One of the main exceptions to this administrative approach to the charter was Article X. Borden submitted that it *should be struck out or materially amended*.[51] What worried Borden and others, besides the points made by Doherty about obligations, was the absence of a crystal ball and the inability to forecast what might happen. A worrying comment from Borden's memorandum was: *There may be national aspirations to which the provisions of the peace treaty will not do justice and which cannot be permanently repressed*.[52] Canada did not want to accept that all the territorial arrangements made at Paris and those not surveyed were necessarily just and beneficial for the future.

The irony was that in fighting for its own autonomy, Canada now appeared to be making unlimited guarantees, and this level of liability was to rankle with Canadians throughout the inter-war years. Going to war to protect the possessions of other states did not appeal to Borden and his Canadian colleagues in Paris and Borden pressed hard for Article X to be amended. However, these protests fell on stony ground and Borden did not get amendments made. As James Eayrs points out, the Article was seen as 'vital' for France, but clearly 'expendable' by Canada.[53] It appears to serve as an example of Canada not obtaining influence when their ideas conflicted directly with the major Powers. Borden and Doherty's strong opposition to Article X was not communicated to Ottawa and Members of Parliament at the time, and Doherty was also somewhat misleading to the Canadian House of Commons in September 1919 when he told Members '... he had formed the conclusion that Art X recognized a principle, but imposed no obligation on Canada to take any part in a war to maintain the territorial integrity or independence of any other member of the League, unless the Dominion Parliament approved of such a step.'[54] This was a very strange interpretation of the Article and does not seem to be in line with the views of other Powers expressed at Paris. Canadians opposed to Article X at least showed persistence in their opposition, since they reintroduced it for discussion at the League of Nations in 1920, again to no great avail (see next chapter).

The German delegation

Sir Robert Borden witnessed the presentation of the Peace Treaty to the German delegation on 7 May. At Versailles, the German delegation was formally announced to the other delegates. *The Count von Brockdorff-Rantzau,* Borden commented in his diary, *is as thin as a lath and apparently very nervous. The Allied Delegates arose at the entrance of the Germans and Clemenceau also when he spoke, Brockdorff R not at all. His speech was maladroit.*[55] All in all, the Germans gave a very poor impression, but Count von Brockdorff- Rantzau had been suffering from nervous exhaustion and might have won some friends by requesting to remain seated while he spoke, rather than merely doing so when others did not. As it was, *Junker pride or stupidity or tactlessness kept him in his seat without one word of explanation.*[56] The Germans took responsibility for the harsh methods they had employed during the war and expressed a willingness to repair much of the damage done, but von Brockdorff-Rantzau also argued that European nations pursued imperialist policies and had inflicted economic hardship on Germany since the armistice. Borden was not impressed with the German presentation, although he clearly understood the gravity of the occasion. *And so the curtain rang down upon the first scene of the last act of the terrible drama which had occupied the world's stage for nearly five years.*[57]

Sir Robert Borden's departure

By May 1919 Robert Borden had become restless in Paris and very much wanted to get back to the domestic political scene in Ottawa. General Louis Botha of South Africa (Prime Minister of South Africa since 1910) and Lloyd George both tried to persuade Borden to remain, at least until the Germans had signed the Treaty. Lloyd George wrote Borden a nice memorandum in praise of his good work at the conference, but this was of no avail. Plainly, Lloyd George did not bear a grudge at Borden's determination to leave Paris since he had him to a pleasant dinner on 13 May before Borden departed the next day for London. On 18 May Borden boarded the *Aquitania* at Southampton docks, arriving back in Halifax, Nova Scotia on 25 May, and leaving the very next day for Ottawa.

Borden returned to issues of taxes and tariffs, demobilisation and industrial production and industrial unrest. Over time, the House of Commons was to remind him of a passage from the Persian poet, Omar Khayyam:

> Myself when young did eagerly frequent
> Doctor and Saint, and heard great Argument
> About it and about; but evermore
> Came out by the same door as in I went.'[58]

Perhaps Borden was not as desperately required in Ottawa as he had so long thought, a self-reflecting conclusion that pushed him towards retirement.

The signing of the Treaty

Borden's place in the pantheon of top Canadian Prime Ministers arguably hinges on his advancement of sovereignty for Canada. This he did by trying to establish the powers of the Canadian plenipotentiaries at the Paris Peace Conference derived from the Canadian Government. Having achieved dual representation at the Paris Conference, Borden believed the concluding status of Canada would be measured by the fact that Canada signed the treaties. Borden, while in Paris, took the initiative, and despite travelling into new constitutional territory telegraphed the Acting Prime Minister in Ottawa, Sir Thomas White: *Under international practice their [Canadian plenipotentiaries] Full Powers are issued by the King but such issuance should be based upon formal action by Canadian Government authorising it.*[59]

Despite the ability of the Canadian Government to pass an Order in Council allowing Canada to sign the treaties and conventions of the Peace Conference 'in the name of His Majesty the King in respect of the Dominion of Canada', this was only possible if the King was moved to request them to do so. In essence, Canada had to get permission of the King to sign the treaties, although the Canadian Government made it sound like a demand. 'Therefore His Excellency the Governor in Council, on the recommendation of the Secretary of State for External Affairs, is pleased to order and doth hereby order that His Majesty the King be humbly moved to issue Letters Patent to each of the following named persons [Borden, Foster, Sifton and Doherty].' It could be said that this was confirmed because the Prime Minister had left no room for discretion over the issue, but J Pope, Undersecretary of State for External Affairs, commented on the draft Order in Council: 'I do not consider that this advice to His Majesty should be couched in this Mandatory form.'[60] That the Secretary of State for External Affairs (Borden) 'doth hereby order' was hardly asking permission of the monarch. However, full authority was issued by His Majesty the King to the Prime Minister of Canada.

The signing of the Peace Treaty in itself takes on some significance since the Dominions sign under the general heading of 'The British Empire'. Further, the order of the signing appears to make Canada and the other Dominions redundant. The British representatives signed for the British Empire and the King, thus the further signatures of the Dominions and India might appear redundant. This was not the view of Borden, and he was to reflect: *In its final form, as amended and incorporated in the Treaty of Peace with Germany, the Covenant fully recognizes the status of the Dominions. As signatories of the Treaty they became members of the League; and their position as to membership and representation in the Assembly is in all respects the same as that of other signatory members.*[61] Borden's own conclusion was that: *During the past six months some notable pages have been written in the constitutional development of our Empire.*[62]

During the past six months some notable pages have been written in the constitutional development of our Empire.

ROBERT BORDEN TO DAVID LLOYD GEORGE, 13 MAY 1919

On 28 June, the treaty was signed in the Hall of Mirrors at the Palace of Versailles. It was, by most accounts, an anticlimax. Although celebrations took place in Paris, there was little ceremony at the signing. The Hall of Mirrors was crowded with statesmen, some reporters and a small number of military personnel. Only brief opening comments were delivered by the Premier of France, Georges Clemenceau, followed by the signing of the treaty by two Germans, Hermann Müller (Secretary for Foreign Affairs) and Johannes Bell (Minister of Transport). The events were brief and did not have the uneasiness that Borden described at the earlier presentation of the treaty to Count von Brockdorff-Rantzau. President Wilson signed as the first of the Allied delegates, followed by his own delegation, which was followed in similar vein by David Lloyd George and the British delegates. The Dominions followed led by the Canadian signatories, Charles Joseph Doherty and Arthur Lewis Sifton. There was no great pageantry and most of the delegates were dressed in civilian clothes and went unrecognised by the audience.

Prime Minister Borden made it clear to the British Government in June 1919 that the Parliament of Canada was required to ratify the peace treaty with Germany, causing a brief diplomatic crisis. Given that the Canadian Parliament would not meet until the autumn, could and should the ratification of the treaty depend upon the pleasure of the Canadian government? Arthur Balfour, British Foreign Secretary, wrote to Viscount Milner, Secretary of State for the Colonies, on 23 July 1919: 'For various reasons the only three powers who are in a position to ratify quickly are France, Italy and Great Britain … It would be disastrous if whole of Peace of the world were to be hung up for months because Canadian Parliament had adjourned and in order to give time for Treaty to reach Australia.'[63]

Fortunately, this memorandum did not prove to be accurate in that it was not until October that France and Italy ratified the treaty. Canada ratified the Versailles treaty by 12 September 1919 – acknowledged in an Order in Council. What initially appeared to be an intolerable delay to the treaty ratification process voiced by Lloyd George and the Colonial Office, proved to work itself out in an amicable way. Milner wrote to Lloyd George: 'This is rather a triumph, as by waiting we have avoided any friction or soreness with the Dominions, while the British Empire is after all ready to ratify as soon as any of the Allies.'[64] The impression was given that diplomatic harmony existed between the Dominions and Great Britain.

The Anglo-French treaty signed on the same day as the Treaty of Versailles (in Paris on 28 June 1919) acknowledged that ratification was required by the Parliaments of the respective Dominions. Other relevant treaties were signed on behalf of Canada by the Canadian High Commissioner in London, Sir George Perley: the Treaty of Neuilly with Bulgaria (November 1919), the Treaty of Trianon with Hungary (June 1920) and the Treaty of Sèvres with Turkey (August 1920). The Treaty of Saint-Germaine-en-Laye (September 1919) with Austria was signed by Sir Edward Kemp.[65]

It was Borden's stately speech that was most memorable from the debates in the Canadian House of Commons on the Treaty of Versailles: *Her [Canada's] resolve had given inspiration, her sacrifices had been conspicuous, her effort was unabated to the end. The same indomitable spirit which made her capable of that effort and sacrifice made her equally incapable of accepting at the Peace Conference, in the League of Nations, or elsewhere, a status inferior to that accorded to nations less advanced in their development, less amply endowed in wealth, resources and population, no more complete in their sovereignty and far less conspicuous in their sacrifice.*[66]

Yet, there was criticism in Parliament of the Treaty of Versailles and the achievements that were being attached to it by

Borden and others. As the Liberal Member of Parliament W S Fielding was to posit, what appeared to have been achieved was the break-up of the British Empire. 'There cannot be two parliamentary governments of equal authority in the Empire.'[67] Stacey comments on the differing views expressed in the debate: 'There was no sign of a national consensus and certainly none of a non-partisan or bi-partisan approach to external problems. It was a moment of great party bitterness, and the Liberal opposition, fresh from the heady experience of a national convention, had no intention of allowing the government any slightest meed of praise for what had been done in Paris.'[68]

Although Canada might appear to have received the recognition it desired, very few could claim glory from the Versailles settlements. Neither Europe nor the world were protected from future wars. An unhappy compromise was struck between the aims of the victorious powers of the First World War, and Germany was left with a considerable sense of grievance. Lloyd George and the British were associated with promoting conciliation rather than just punishment. Canada could not solve the world's problems, only receive recognition within it.

Borden's role at Versailles

Strong arguments exist that Robert Borden should not be considered as the key to Canada's international autonomy in the inter-war years. Rather than Borden, it was the Canadian dead at Ypres, Vimy Ridge and Passchendaele that changed attitudes inside and outside Canada towards how Canada should be treated on the international stage. The wartime contribution could not be ignored, even by a United States with a dislike for the British Empire. Canada's contribution to the First World War from the very beginning of the call to arms stood in contrast to the late entry of the United States into the conflict. This had given Canada a serious stake in the Paris Peace Conference and important issues like reparations. As Frederic Soward put it, 'It was Canadian blood which purchased the title deeds to Canadian autonomy in foreign affairs.'[69]

'It was Canadian blood which purchased the title deeds to Canadian autonomy in foreign affairs.'

FREDERIC H SOWARD, HISTORIAN, CANADIAN HISTORICAL ASSOCIATION BOOKLET, 1956

Borden was also not alone among Dominion leaders in seeking a more advanced foreign policy role for the individual states within the British Empire and Dominions. The contribution of General Jan Christian Smuts was equally important for Dominion autonomy; his contribution certainly arose back at the Imperial War Conference of 1917, and Borden was happy to acknowledge the significant contribution of the South African in Resolution IX at the 1917 conference.

Canada's signature on the Peace Treaty at Versailles can also be considered a bit of a deception; it was under a British Empire heading. For all of the grandstanding of Borden about obtaining a separate Canadian signature and signatures on the Paris treaties, this was little more than window-dressing. The fact that the United States did not ratify the treaties made this kind of symbolism rather weak. Important Powers make important decisions.

Consensus politics, ultimately among the Big Three (United Kingdom, United States and France), prevailed at Paris. How many representatives each country had was irrelevant. All the time that was spent on representation became meaningless when it was the consensus of the Big Five, Big

Four and ultimately the Big Three nations that actually mattered. Canada did not win membership of the committee that created the League of Nations. While it participated in discussions concerned with the Japanese on the equality clause to the Covenant of the League, its arguments did not prevail. On the settlement on Germany, Canada, like other less significant powers, had little impact, although on reparations it took a strong interest.

Yet Canada behaved as an 'international person' at Paris: Borden deputised for Lloyd George, represented the British Empire delegation at some Council of Five sessions and attended a number of Council of Four meetings to deal with issues of economic matters, waterways and railways, and submarine cables.[70] He also chaired some of the British Empire delegation meetings in Paris.

Back home, Canada's participation at the Paris Peace Conference was made a matter of public and press concern: something serious had to be delivered and was.[71] It could not be taken for granted at the end of the First World War that the Dominions would be sitting in an international post-war peace conference. Borden had to argue very strongly for this, and made sure the Canadian voice was heard in London and subsequently Paris. Canadians expected no less, but it was not within their own gift.

Being part of such a monumental event as the Paris Peace Conference gave Sir Robert Borden and his colleagues access to many significant individuals, including David Lloyd George, Woodrow Wilson and Georges Clemenceau. It supplied Canada with information; they discovered what was going on and why. Lloyd George would write of Borden that he was: 'a sagacious and helpful counsellor, never forgetting that his first duty was to the people of the great Dominion he represented, but also realizing that they were engaged in an imperial enterprise and that an insistent and obstructive particularism would destroy any hope of achieving success in the common task.'[72] The success of their relationship was that they drew on each other's talents; Lloyd George had more new ideas than Borden, but Borden was good at getting things done.

Borden was '... the very quintessence of common sense. Always calm, well-balanced, a man of co-operating temper, invariably subordinating self to the common cause, he was a sagacious and helpful counsellor, never forgetting that his first duty was to the people of the great Dominion he represented, but also realizing that they were engaged in an imperial enterprise and that an insistent and obstructive particularism would destroy any hope of achieving success in the common task.'

DAVID LLOYD GEORGE, *WAR MEMOIRS*, VOL IV (1934)

While obtaining the authority for Canada to sign the Paris treaties can be viewed as insignificant, in that signatures are merely imprints on pieces of paper, the legal weight attached to signature of the treaties would help to determine a rational legal approach to international affairs. It was Borden and the Canadian delegation who won the right to sign the Paris Peace Settlements, cajoling the British Government and even bullying the king to get what they wanted.

Borden was determined that the ratification process should include the Canadian Parliament, despite pressure from the British and even if a delay initially embarrassed the British Government. He wanted Parliament to decide in a way that would be echoed by Prime Minister Mackenzie King twenty years later at the outbreak of the Second World War. Mackenzie King, like Borden, emphasised the sovereignty of Parliament in key foreign policy decisions. The Canadian Parliament ratified the Treaty of Versailles in September 1919.

In the League of Nations, Canada would be represented individually. Canada moved to the 'high table' of representation and provided delegates to both the League of Nations and the International Labour Organisation. There were still Great Powers after the Versailles settlements were agreed (it was not expected to be otherwise) and the League of Nations was to appear rather Eurocentric in its policies, but Canada was there. Canada could even make mistakes in diplomacy in the inter-war years; it had won the right to do so.

Canada's international status, however difficult to define at times, had changed as a consequence of participation at the Versailles Peace Conference and the manner of that participation. Canada's national interest was not seen as incompatible with Empire: for Sir Robert Borden Canadian autonomy had its own parameters. For Canada and Borden, British imperialism and Canadian nationalism were not necessarily irreconcilable; and Borden, as a consequence of decisions relating to the Paris Peace Conference, believed he could influence both.

Sir Robert Borden and elder statesman in 1930

III

The Legacy

6

The Early Post-war Years

Ratification of the Treaty of Versailles in Canada and the move towards Canadian diplomatic representation in Washington meant Borden had accomplished much since the end of the First World War. But the war and the Conference had taken their toll on Borden's health and emotional state, and he offered his resignation as Prime Minister to the Cabinet on 16 December 1919. His doctor had advised him to resign, but the Cabinet pressed him to stay on in the post of Prime Minister but take a 'sabbatical' for a year, and he agreed. Despite vacations he found his state of health made it unwise to continue as Prime Minister, however, and on 10 July the following year he held his last Cabinet meeting. He remained a Member of Parliament until the 1921 general election, but even then was not finished with public life or international concerns.

Despite the international status that Canada appeared to attain at the Paris Peace Conference, there was little immediate change to Canadian foreign policy. A clear definition of the relationship between the Dominions and Great Britain would have to wait until 1926. As Margaret MacMillan points out, Canada did not 'show much interest in the round of conferences and meetings that followed Paris. It sent only a token delegation to the important Genoa economic conference in 1922 and was not represented at all at the Lausanne conference of 1923 that finally made peace between the Allies and the new Turkey.'[1] International reality took a while to recognise the change in Canadian attitudes and those of other Dominions. The Balfour Declaration of 1926 and the Statute of Westminster of 1931 would implement the nature and language of a Commonwealth that was apparent in Canadian foreign policy in 1919.

Sir Victor Christian William Cavendish, ninth Duke of Devonshire (1868–1938) was Governor General of Canada, 1916–21. On becoming Duke of Devonshire in 1908, he inherited Chatsworth House in Derbyshire. It was during the First World War that he was appointed to be Governor General, in mildly controversial circumstances. Cavendish was appointed by the king on the recommendation of Prime Minister Herbert Asquith, without any consultation with Robert Borden. Sir George Perley, Canadian High Commissioner to the United Kingdom, was informed by Borden of his disquiet at not being asked to approve the appointment. However, Borden became happy to have the Duke of Devonshire as the new Governor General and found him very co-operative.

Canada did not yet have the diplomats or expertise to seize the opportunities the Paris Peace Conference had arguably afforded it. After the ratification of the Treaty of Versailles by the Canadian Parliament, Borden turned his attention to diplomatic representation in Washington. Oddly, in February 1919, Borden had been offered the position of British Ambassador to the United States by Lloyd George. He was willing to give it consideration in due course and admitted *the position was one that I should have been willing to accept if political conditions permitted.*[2] Embarrassingly, the matter appeared in the press before it had been adequately discussed and a decision made. Consequently, Borden announced on 26 March that he would not take the position.

What Borden was really after was the establishment of a full Canadian legation in the United States; he had pressed Lloyd George on this as early as March 1919, wanting Canadian representation at Washington, but also more information from the British Embassy there on industrial, commercial and political matters that affected Canada.

Intriguingly, the Governor General of Canada made it apparent that as he did not wish to censor sensitive material from the British Embassy in Washington and be seen to be withholding it from Canadian ministers, sensitive information should not be sent to him.[3] Canada was not, therefore, quite getting the transparency in communications that it asked for. In 1919 and 1920, an array of diplomatic correspondence passed between Washington, Ottawa and London on the issue of Canadian diplomatic representation in Washington, and that a Canadian minister should represent Canada in the United States. Although this was agreed, the new minister was perceived to be taking his orders from the British Ambassador as well as the Secretary of State for External Affairs in Ottawa. Altogether it was a rather clumsy compromise, but indicative of the fact that the Canadian Government apparently still saw the necessity of a shared imperial foreign policy. Strangely, too, the appointment did not actually come into effect until 1927, when Vincent Massey took up the post. Borden's enthusiasm for a new post in Washington was not shared by his immediate successors.

In March 1920 the United States Senate rejected taking up membership of the League of Nations; for many, this made the League's prospects for success limited, if not impossible. The history of this difficult, ironic and ultimately disastrous state of affairs has been related elsewhere, and will not be dwelled upon here, except to the extent this was perceived by Sir Robert Borden and Canada. Over a year after the Senate rejection, Borden ruminated on the issue with British statesman Arthur Balfour, and appeared to blame President Woodrow Wilson for the failure of the United States to join the League of Nations: *With all his great qualities President Wilson possessed a temperament that unfortunately prevented him from inviting or even accepting the co-operation of his political opponents, he could not stoop to conquer.* Borden was also pessimistic about the future prospect of the United States joining the League, continuing, *Unfortunately the United States has declined membership in the League, and thus its association and co-operation, which are so important, can hardly be realised through that instrumentality. I do not believe in the probability, or even the possibility, for many years to come of securing a two-thirds majority of the United States Senate to approve the Covenant.*[4] On the whole, however, members of the Canadian Government held a more positive view, and hoped the US would join the League at some future date. If the United States did join, it would bring some needed world perspective and international coherence to the work and organisation of the League.

The United States' absence from the League of Nations reflected and fuelled domestic isolationist elements within it and also within Canada. For Canada, this meant that the issue of imperial relations counted for less, and it also encouraged the country to revisit Article X of the League's Covenant. This article was in fact one of the reasons why the United States had come to find the Covenant of the League of Nations objectionable. The strong irony was that at Paris the United States had argued vociferously for it. Originally, of course, Doherty had put forward proposals to delete Article X. Now, the Canadian position had changed, and Canadians opposed to Article X hoped that the fact Article X had kept the United States out of the League of Nations, which they presented as a dire situation, would encourage other members of the League of Nations to reconsider the issue. However, it was a little premature to expect League members to dismantle something that had just been created; and in the end, the Canadian delegates did not secure the support of even one member of the Committee on Amendments to the Covenant of the League of Nations.[5]

The Canadian League delegates were not, however, willing to let sleeping dogs lie; although little might be gained from pursuing the issue of Article X further, they did so anyway. What they subsequently sought was no longer a deletion of the article, but an amendment that might allow interpretation in their favour. What they essentially aimed to do was to take away the obligations of nation-states that could be considered to be geographically disassociated from a crisis area to support an invaded member country. By September 1923, the League of Nations Council was willing to reconsider interpretation of Article X, even if linguistically it did not change. The Canadian resolution received support from 29 states, with 22 abstentions and only Persia voting against.[6] Since a unanimous vote was required, this meant the proposal had been defeated, yet Canada felt its resolution had been 'approved' and should Article X be invoked, their interpretation would be followed. Thus, as Richard Veatch points out, ended this long Canadian struggle 'on a note of ambiguity'.[7]

Washington Naval Conference, 1921–2

After almost nine years as Prime Minister, Borden retired in 1920, aged 66, although he remained as a Member of Parliament until December 1921. Robert and Laura remained at their home Glensmere at 201 Wurtenberg Street, Ottawa, having not retained many connections to Halifax. As with many politicians in retirement, Borden continued to write and lecture, delivering the Marfleet lectures at the University of Toronto and the Rhodes lectures at the University of Oxford in 1922 and 1927, respectively. Being a man who was always sensible in the use of his money and with clever investments, his income exceeded his expenditure during his retirement. In 1928, Borden accepted the presidencies of the Crown Life Insurance Company and Barclays Bank (Canada).

Sir Robert Borden's impact on international affairs was to continue as he entered a period as an elder statesman of Canada with an international reputation. He was invited to be on the Committee of Amendments to the Covenant of the League of Nations, but declined. However, he did not decline all invitations to involve himself in international affairs. His reputation as an international statesman was enough to see him appointed as the Canadian representative to the Washington Naval Conference from 11 November 1921 to February 1922. The conference, as the invitation to the British Government in London stated, would cover 'the subject of limitation of armaments, in connection with which Pacific and Far Eastern questions will also be discussed'.[8]

The United States President, Warren G Harding, had not sent separate invitations to the Dominions, although it has been argued that the State Department had a full expectation that there would be a delegation representing Great Britain and the Dominions.[9] The British wisely determined they would send a British Empire delegation similar to that sent to Paris in 1919 and the British Colonial Secretary on behalf of the Prime Minister, David Lloyd George, wrote to the Canadian Governor General to invite a Canadian participant.

Alongside Canada were Australia, New Zealand and India. South Africa did not send a delegate, but the South African Prime Minister was mindful to tell the Canadian Prime Minister that the Dominions should receive a separate invitation to the conference from the United States. Smuts was concerned the United States was rather dismissive of Dominion status and since this was the first international conference since the Paris Peace Conference, the opportunity needed to be seized to establish equality of status. However, the 'horse had left the stable' on this issue; the invitation had already been sent to Great Britain and not individual Dominions, and to raise the issue at this stage would have largely just achieved the animosity of the United States. The lack of a separate invitation to Canada from the United States could have been seen as an affront to Canada's standing as of equal international status. Lloyd George, however, confirmed that representation by the Dominions was on the same basis as the Paris Peace Conference, promising, 'Effect of this will be that signature of each Dominion delegate will be necessary in addition to signature of British delegates to commit British Empire delegation as a whole to any agreements made at Conference, and that any Dominion delegate can reserve assent on behalf of his Government if he wishes.'[10]

Sir Robert Borden was thus asked by Canadian Prime Minister Arthur Meighen (Prime Minister for the short period 10 July to 29 December 1921) to represent Canada at the conference. The stalwart legal adviser Loring Christie was appointed to the secretariat and accompanied Borden to Washington. Britain was represented by former Prime Minister Arthur Balfour, who appeared to get on with Borden extremely well. Balfour was given a fairly free hand in the negotiations, not having been given detailed instructions from the British Cabinet. Lloyd George did not attend the conference himself because he was preoccupied at home with the Irish Home Rule question and economic circumstances related to unemployment.

The conference comprised 26 meetings of the five significant naval powers (the United States, the British Empire, Japan, France and Italy) and China, Portugal, the Netherlands and Belgium. In the context of limiting naval armaments the agenda of the conference was quite broad. Not only did it include the basis and extent of limitation but also Pacific and Far Eastern questions relating to China.

The chair of the British Empire delegation was taken in rotation by the delegates, and Borden took his turn. The function of the British Empire delegation was to respond to various proposals already put forward. The *New York Evening Post* of 18 November 1921 captured the position of Sir Robert Borden in an interesting way: 'Among people of all parties in Canada there is general confidence that Sir Robert Borden will not allow the Dominion's special viewpoint and interests to be swamped because Downing Street favours some particular policy. By reason of his long political career and his extensive experience in imperial and international affairs gained at various conferences held in recent years, Sir Robert ought, after Mr Balfour, to be the most influential member of the British delegation and while he may not make any spectacular speeches, his voice will carry great weight in the inner councils.'[11]

The Washington Naval Conference, which was concerned with more than just naval disarmament, can be likened to the Paris Peace Conference, in that the main work of Canada was done on its sub-committees. In the case of Paris in 1919, Borden became an expert on Greek-Albanian borders; in the case of Washington in 1921–2, his talents were directed to Chinese customs tariffs. Borden became the principal delegate to draft what can only be seen as a subordinate issue of the conference, but to his credit a Nine-Power Treaty relating to Chinese tariffs did take effect.

As a result of a general election in Canada on 6 December 1921, Prime Minister Meighen was out of office before the Washington Conference was concluded. The Conservatives were blamed for conscription and won only 50 of the 235 seats in Parliament. Meighen was even defeated in his own electoral riding. The Liberal Party, with 116 seats, were just short of a majority of seats in Parliament. The new Prime Minister was William Lyon Mackenzie King. Borden was apprehensive about whether or not he would still be required by Mackenzie King as conference delegate: *As you are about to assume the Premiership I naturally have to consider whether my presence at Washington as representative of Canada may not embarrass you. It is hardly necessary to say that if you should desire to have our country represented here by some one more thoroughly in your confidence than I can claim to be, I will most gladly relinquish my present duties, which indeed I did not seek, and which I accepted rather reluctantly.*[12] Mackenzie King was, however, determined to keep Borden in his position to see the Conference through to its conclusion; Borden was far more qualified for the job than Mackenzie King himself.

The famous feature of the conference is that it led to the abandonment of the Anglo-Japanese Alliance (in existence in some form since 1902 and up for review in 1921), which had existed to combat a perceived Russian menace and then a German threat. If these issues were no longer prominent then the utility of the Anglo-Japanese Alliance was brought into question. Canada felt quite strongly that the Anglo-Japanese

Alliance should be replaced. The abandonment of the alliance led to a Four-Power Treaty (between the British Empire, Japan, France and the United States dealing with territorial possession of these powers in the Pacific region) and a Five-Power Treaty (between the British Empire, France, Italy, Japan and the United States of America, for the Limitation of Naval Armament). The Five-Power Treaty famously put restrictions on the replacement tonnage of battleships (ratios of 5:5:3 for the United States, Britain and Japan and 1.75:1.75 for France and Italy) and a 10-year prohibition on battleship construction. The arming of certain ships was limited in the calibre of guns they could host. Most of this was at the suggestion of the United States Secretary of State, Charles Evans Hughes, with the support of Robert Borden. Despite Canada not having battleships of its own, and not providing any meaningful support towards the naval strength of the Empire, Borden spoke in favour of the proposition of the United States.[13] The ratio for Great Britain applied to the combined navies of the British Empire and Dominions, and thus in essence they were left to decide themselves the distribution of forces and the quotas that each would retain.

Borden wrote to Ottawa on 14 November 1921 showing his support for the policy of Hughes over the moratorium on the building of battleships: ... *this feature of the American proposal appeals most strongly to the great mass of the people, and that it would be most unfortunate if the British Empire should not give a wholehearted acceptance of the principle thus put forward.*[14] The proposal also had the full support of the Australian delegate, G F Pearce. When Borden sought permission on 10 December to sign one of the early agreements of the conference on behalf of Canada, this was freely granted by Prime Minister Meighen. In fact, this was given even before he read the official draft of the treaty: 'Replying your telegram tenth draft treaty has not reached me nor has an extended report appeared in Press here, but if Friday *New York Times* correctly indicates substance thereof you are authorized to sign on behalf of Canada.'[15] However reliable *The New York Times* might have been, this seemed an odd way to conduct serious international affairs.

When Mackenzie King came to office, he expected to confer directly with Borden before he signed naval treaties on behalf of Canada. When it initially looked as if Borden would not return to Ottawa before the treaty would need to be signed, Mackenzie King made it clear to Borden that the treaty should not be signed if it contravened any of the provisions of the Canadian Naval Service Act of 1910. 'With regard to any other treaties you may be expected to sign,' he continued, 'if in any particular they are likely to be a matter of special concern to Canada as affecting the relations of the Dominion with other parts of the British Empire or with other countries, I should like it to be expressed that the treaty as signed on behalf of Canada is subject to approval of the Canadian Parliament.'[16]

In fact, the Four-Power Naval Treaty that was signed on the 13 December was a treaty between the British Empire, France, Japan and the United States of America relating to their insular possessions and insular dominions in the Pacific Ocean (insular meaning those areas that were geographically separated or isolated), that had no relationship with the Naval Service Act of 1910. Canada was only affected by the treaties discussed at Washington if the whole of the British Empire was made more vulnerable as a consequence of these decisions. Borden reminded Mackenzie King that, of course, all treaties signed at the Washington Conference were subject to the ratification by the Canadian Parliament, as had been the case with the Paris treaties.[17]

Given the sensitivity of Canada's constitutional position with regard to the British Empire and what it meant for Borden to put his signature on a treaty, Mackenzie King was not satisfied. He strongly believed the Canadian Government should approve the treaties before they were given to the Canadian Parliament for approval, and that Borden's signature should only be seen as conditional. It is not clear if Borden found these exchanges in any way tiresome, but the constitutional position of Canada in the international community was important to him, as was the importance of his signature on a treaty. He would have been the last person to want to usurp Canadian sovereignty vested in the Canadian Government. Borden replied to Mackenzie King that the treaty contained the clear statement before the signatures that the treaty needed to be ratified in line with the constitutional provisions within the individual states: : … *the Treaty would not be binding upon Canada unless it is ratified in accordance with the constitutional methods in force in Canada … it will be for the Canadian Government to determine the character of these constitutional methods in force in Canada … the modern constitutional practice as I understand it is to submit treaties of this character for the approval of Parliament before they are ratified by the Government.*[18]

The abandonment of the Anglo-Japanese Alliance and the reality of Britain's declining naval power would have repercussions for the future. More immediately, Borden saw events as reflecting the development of a foreign policy of the British Empire based on consultation. The conference had shown that Britain and Canada were less concerned with offending Japan than they were with the United States. The Japanese, despite the ratio restrictions, did quite well out of the status quo being accepted in the Pacific, giving them a rather significant sphere of influence. When Japan became aggressive in the 1930s, the systemic weaknesses of the Washington system became apparent.

Interestingly, the signing of the treaties delivered at Washington followed a similar line to that of the Paris Peace Conference. The delegates of Great Britain signed under His Majesty's titles, and were followed by Sir Robert Borden for Canada and the other Dominion representatives present.

During the conference Borden had found time to reply to a letter from a student at Columbia University, New York, who was writing a dissertation on 'Canada as a Political Entity'. One of the student's mildly impertinent questions concerned how Borden was appointed and whether or not a Canadian was at the conference 'because the Government of Great Britain thought it expedient, and thus chose a Canadian as a matter of courtesy, or by reason of that Canadian's ability?'[19] He bravely continued: 'My query is whether the method of appointment of delegates to the Washington Conference has been such as to impair the Canadian rights acknowledged by the Versailles precedent?'[20] Borden's reply to Alex Potter on 8 December 1921 was surprisingly cordial under the circumstances and appeared to clarify the matter: *The position of the Dominion representative at the Washington Conference is the same as it was at the Paris Peace Conference. Each one was appointed by the King on the advice of the Dominion Government expressed through a Dominion Order in Council. Any agreement reached at the Conference must, in order to bind the whole British Empire, be signed by the Dominion representatives on behalf of their respective Dominions as well as by the British representatives on behalf of Great Britain.*[21]

Canada's international status and the League of Nations

The early diplomatic lessons of the Washington Conference appeared to have been learned by the British by the time of the Genoa conference of April and May 1922 dealing with post-war economic, financial and political recovery, and organised by the Italians. Although a separate invitation was sent by the Italian government to Canada, it was Lloyd George who was behind the direct invitations to the Dominions.[22] The representatives from Canada were Sir Charles Blair Gordon, a manufacturer and banker, and Professor Edouard Montpetit, an economist. The only major instructions they were given by Mackenzie King were to avoid involvement in questions that related just to Europe and confine themselves to an interest in issues of a direct economic concern to Canada. Although very little appeared to be achieved by the Genoa conference, in a rather typical way, this suited Mackenzie King; Canada's international recognition had been improved and Canada had no further responsibilities as a consequence. Short of entangling military alliances, Borden had wanted a greater involvement for Canada in international affairs than was being practiced at Genoa. Mackenzie King was more cautious and isolationist.

One of the consequences for Canada of the Treaty of Versailles and the Covenant of the League of Nations was the further requirement to define Canadian nationality. Every potential member state of the League of Nations was required to define the nationality of its citizens. An Act of the Canadian Parliament of 1921 defined two categories of Canadian citizens: native Canadians and British subjects who also had a distinct status as Canadian citizens. Although international law may be hazy, this Canadian move allowed for a clearer definition of a Canadian national. Canada, as a member of the League of Nations, was able to appoint two Canadian nationals as members of the Permanent Court of International Justice.[23]

Canada's support for the League of Nations and the Permanent Court of International Justice was strong, even if its support for collective security was rather qualified. It believed international disputes should be submitted to arbitration and the good offices of the international court could come into play as appropriate. In fact, Canada was happy to support the jurisdiction of the Permanent Court of International Justice as having binding international authority.

Canada was also aware of the limitations of the League of Nations, and, as indicated earlier, remained concerned about the commitments inherent in Article X of the Covenant and the absence of the United States. The Canadian Government continued to hope that the United States would work very closely with the League, as it also did for Germany and the Soviet Union, both of which would join the League separately later. Yet Canada became rather isolationist in the inter-war years and the League of Nations was not championed in Canada for an ability to enforce peace, but for its potential for conciliation. Why should Canada go to war in Europe over rather badly created borders that raised as many difficulties about national self-determination as it solved?

The Chanak incident

A test of the nature of consultation between Great Britain and Canada came with a crisis in Turkey in 1922. Canadian historian Robert MacGregor Dawson suggests: 'The efforts which had been made during the preceding few years to develop a centralized control of Empire foreign policy were suddenly rendered useless, the idea of joint responsibility in foreign affairs was badly shaken, and opposing tendencies in different parts of the Empire became dramatically apparent.'[24]

How did this come about? Although the Treaty of Sèvres of August 1920, which divided much of the Ottoman Empire in the interests of Great Britain, France, Italy and Greece, had been signed by the Allies as one of the treaties of the Paris settlements, it was not ratified by Great Britain and was denounced by a Nationalist Government in Turkey. The treaty tried to settle Turkey's frontiers concerning Greece, the Black Sea, and the Sea of Marmara with Syria, Mesopotamia, Persia and Russia. One major feature of the treaty was the internationalization of the Black Sea Straits or Dardanelles (the strait between the Aegean Sea and the Sea of Marmara). The navigation of the Straits would be kept open in periods of peace or war and certain ports were seen as neutral including Constantinople, Smyrna (İzmir), Alexandretta and Haifa. Constantinople, the Black Sea Straits and the town of Chanak (a small garrison town on the Turkish coast held by the British) became flashpoints of dissension for the Turks as they entered the neutral zone under administration of the British and threatened the neutrality of the Straits. The British, with some agreement between Churchill and Lloyd George, were willing to fight to prevent the spread of Turkish influence and power. Churchill was concerned about the consequences 'in India and among other Mohammedan populations for which we are responsible'.[25] He continued in this vein, five days later, in a further telegram to the Governor General of Canada (a way the Colonial Secretary was passing information from the British to the Canadian Prime Minister), in which he reviewed the situation: 'There is a general tendency to loss of morale among the Christian Powers in regard to Eastern question but a quiet demonstration of firmness on our part supported by Dominion Governments should be decisive.'[26] Churchill and Lloyd George were looking for verbal support from Canada, a support that would state Canada was prepared to send troops.

The Chanak Crisis illustrated rather well that if a crisis arose in the affairs of the British Empire, adequate diplomatic and political machinery did not exist to deal with it. The Prime Ministers' Conference of 1921 had not anticipated this crisis, a system of consultation between Britain and senior Dominion figures was not otherwise evident and the information the Dominions received from Great Britain did not include detailed Near East reports that allowed them to feel informed.[27]

The story gets more complicated for Canada because Winston Churchill (British Colonial Secretary) made a public appeal to the unity of the British Empire on the issue before the Canadian Prime Minister, Mackenzie King, had been consulted. Churchill wanted to muster as much Dominion support as he could as quickly as possible. This haste was to prove a problem. Also, the delay in communication (a formal telegram was sent to Ottawa on 15 September 1922) could be seen as unfortunate and unlucky; the concluding two sentences of the telegram read: 'The announcement that all or any of the Dominions were prepared to send contingents even of moderate size would undoubtedly in itself exercise a most favourable influence on the situation and might conceivably be a potent factor in preventing actual hostilities. This telegram has also been sent to the Governors General of Commonwealth of Australia, New Zealand and Union of South Africa.'[28]

In asking for announcements of support, Churchill had put pressure on the Dominions in the public domain, a pressure increased when Churchill and Lloyd George told the press they had requested assistance. Confidentiality and diplomacy seemed to have disappeared over this crisis. Mackenzie King was away from Ottawa in his constituency at the time the decoded telegram was sent to him, but the delay in deciphering the long telegram meant Churchill was rather premature and over-enthusiastic in briefing the press in Britain. The fact that the Canadian Prime Minister learned of what appeared to be a British request for arms and solidarity from a Canadian newspaperman was not only highly embarrassing; it appeared that the press had been used by the British Government to usurp the authority of the Dominion Governments.

The Chanak Crisis fizzled out rather than exploded, the incidents on the Black Sea Straits proved to be not too serious and, after agreeing to transfer Eastern Thrace and Istanbul to Mustafa Kemal (later Atatürk) and his forces and the evacuation of the Greeks from the territories, an armistice was rather quickly agreed. It appeared Churchill had been more concerned about the support of Australia and New Zealand in the Near East than the involvement of Canada. Nevertheless, the damage had been done to Canadian pride and how Canada might procedurally be drawn into another war was not clear. The conclusion was drawn that the common decentralised Empire policy promoted by Sir Robert Borden had failed in an early test case. However, the crisis was not seen as forming any complete precedent and Mackenzie King did not immediately demand complete control of all Canadian foreign policy, although this would come.

Mackenzie King had shown that his own well-organised indecision managed to diffuse the situation. In making a constitutional crisis out of the events, Mackenzie King could avoid the decision about providing assistance. Also, he could take the high ground of indignation and present the issue as a crisis in British politics rather than Canadian. Churchill sent his own muted apology to Mackenzie King: 'If, as we may hope, we are approaching the end of this crisis, I trust I may once more venture to ask you to make every allowance in case of any defect in the procedure for the sudden emergency which arose and the need of firm and instant action at a time when our Allies were prepared to take everything lying down and when we were confronted single handed with the headlong advance of the Turk.'[29] Mackenzie King could later exploit the fact that he had had little consultation prior to the crisis and that despatches from Great Britain about the Near East had been entirely inadequate.

Arthur Meighen, Opposition leader, was to take a Conservative Party line that evoked the famous words of the popular Liberal Prime Minister of the past, Wilfred Laurier: 'There are those who write and talk as though Britain were not our good partner and friend but our chief antagonist, an imperious, designing mistress, seeking to lead us to our ruin ... Let there be no dispute as to where I stand. When Britain's message came then Canada should have said: Ready, aye ready; we stand by you.'[30]

The effects of the Chanak Crisis on Great Britain can be seen as being somewhat more immediate and dramatic; Lloyd George was ousted from office as Prime Minister. The likelihood of his being able to lead a coalition government after a general election diminished because of the hostile press and opposition from Members of Parliament over the incident in Turkey. He resigned on 23 October, and Andrew Bonar Law became Prime Minister as head of a Unionist Government.

As a consequence of the Chanak incident and the unresolved issues of the Treaty of Sèvres signed in 1919 relating to Turkey and the Near Eastern crisis, a peace conference was held in Lausanne. It was France that put the 'fly in the ointment' by asking for representation from Algeria, Tunis and West Africa if the Dominion Governments were invited. Although Mackenzie King might have been expected to be upset by not being invited to the Lausanne Peace Conference, he rather strangely was not. Mackenzie King did not want to participate in the conference and felt the Chanak Crisis supported his view that an imperial foreign policy could not function adequately given the immediate problems of communication that had taken place. It exposed the myth of a unified and coherent foreign policy and the Prime Minister of Canada even questioned whether or not integrated diplomacy was possible. Any decisions made at Lausanne would not be considered to be committing Canada. Of course, Mackenzie King was a Canadian Prime Minister who liked to avoid commitments. Nevertheless, the Treaty of Lausanne, signed on 24 July 1923, established the borders of modern Turkey and much else besides; and it is the only one of the treaties signed after the First World War that has survived.

The Imperial Conference of 1923 and US-Canadian foreign policy

The Prime Minister's Conference of 1921 (meetings of representatives of the United Kingdom, the Dominions and India in London) was arranged to allow the discussion of pertinent issues to the Dominions and Britain: renewal of the Anglo-Japanese Alliance, the Soviet Union and the Near East. Canadian documents of the Department of External Affairs refer to the conference as the Prime Ministers' Conference, not as an Imperial Conference; they appear to reserve the latter title for the conference that would discuss constitutional issues desired by the Imperial War Conference of 1917 and held in 1923. Nevertheless, the Prime Ministers' Conference was a prelude to the important Washington Naval Conference of 1921–2, and although we have seen Borden was a representative of Canada in Washington, he was not a participant at London. It was the new Prime Minister, Meighen, who made it clear at the Prime Ministers' Conference that Canada favoured the abandonment of the Anglo-Japanese Alliance. A major reason for the Canadian view was that it wanted the goodwill of China, and more particularly trade with China, a view Canada felt the United States shared and a policy Borden implemented at the Washington Naval Conference. At least the Dominions could feel consulted on this major issue of the Anglo-Japanese Alliance, and this was the type of consultation Borden had previously worked so hard for.

In the wake of the Prime Ministers' Conference and the Washington Naval Conference came the Imperial Conference of 1923 and the Imperial Economic Conference of 1923, which ran concurrently (the Imperial Economic Conference concerned itself with fairly technical economic issues and imperial economic development). Prime Minister Meighen in 1921 had made sure he did not disrupt the nature of the British Empire and did not introduce any major discussion of the devolution of foreign policy powers. In contrast, Prime Minister Mackenzie King, in a rather lengthy statement to the fourth meeting of the Imperial Conference in 1923, emphasized the need for a foreign policy separate from Great Britain. It was becoming apparent that Canada now had a mind of its own in foreign policy matters.

David Lloyd George had made a statement to the British House of Commons in December 1921 which first praised the revolutionary changes in the foreign policies of the Dominions since 1917, but then spoke of the foreign policy of the Empire as being in the control of the British Foreign Office. Mackenzie King's long statement to the Imperial Conference included a retort to this, and he used a quotation from a speech by Sir Clifford Sifton on 'The Political Status of Canada' to make his point: 'This statement is rather startling after Sir John Macdonald and Sir Charles Tupper, Sir Wilfrid Laurier and Sir Robert Borden for 50 years have asserted the right of Canada to have no military or financial responsibility for a war, unless her Parliament voluntarily takes on that responsibility. We now find the Prime Minister of Great Britain making the statement that we have entered into an arrangement by which we assume the responsibility for the wars of Great Britain all over the world in return for being consulted ... the Dominions [thus] become jointly responsible for everything the British Foreign Office does in every part of the world.'[31] Mackenzie King strongly endorsed Sifton's conclusion that Canada's commitment to any war would lie entirely with the Canadian Parliament.

One of the main reasons Mackenzie King promoted an independent line from Great Britain in foreign policy matters was because of Canada's very 'independent' relationship with the United States, which had manifested itself in issues of boundaries (passage through the St Lawrence Waterway), joint irrigation, fishing (Canadian-United States Halibut Fisheries Treaty 1923) and tariffs. Also, in a similar way that the western areas of the United States had become important in its domestic politics, the Prairie Provinces were important in Canada, and the two countries had mutual interests in their border territories. It was not difficult to see that the ties and mutual interests of Canada and the United States in the west and mid-west were much stronger than its connections to Europe.

The Halibut Fisheries Treaty was a good example of an area of little direct imperial concern and a predominately commercial concern of Canada and the United States. The depletion of halibut off the Pacific coast of Canada and the United States was seen as a very regional issue and led to the establishment of a 'closed season' prohibiting the fishing of halibut between November and February. The fishing area was so far removed from Great Britain that no British nationals were expected to be involved in fishing in the area. Consequently, Canada negotiated and signed the treaty without the involvement of Great Britain. Although the British Government did not like being overlooked, particularly with any dealings the Canadian Government had with Washington, the Halibut Fisheries Treaty went ahead nevertheless.

In 1922 and 1923 Mackenzie King also tried to revisit the Rush-Bagot Treaty of 1817 that restricted naval armaments on the Great Lakes. It was largely considered an obsolete treaty from a pre-Confederation period, the problems on the Great Lakes by the 1920s being more concerned with policing action. This was again a matter Canada believed was one that concerned itself and the United States rather than being an issue in which Great Britain needed direct involvement. However, the complexities of replacing the existing treaty between Britain and the United States proved to be great and the Canadian Government dropped the idea of introducing a replacement.

At the fourth meeting of the Imperial Conference of 1923, Mackenzie King was keen to suggest to the other delegates that Canada's interests extended around the world, but no real attempt was made to disguise the fact that Canada's interest in the Far East largely related to immigration. It had a peculiar domestic context in that politicians in British Columbia wanted to restrict Japanese immigration. This was reminiscent of the Paris debates over the racial clause in the Covenant of the League of Nations and also Canadian representation on the Council of the International Labour Organisation that Robert Borden had entered into. As Mackenzie King indelicately put it, 'These Orientals have the capacity for increasing their numbers once they get into the country. The children of Japanese and Chinese families on the whole are much more numerous in British Columbia than are the children of white families.' [32] Rather than enforcing prohibition through legislation, Mackenzie King wanted the Japanese to introduce self-regulation. Hence, he called on the co-operation of the British Foreign Minister in Japan for help in limiting Japanese emigration to Canada and consulted a representative of the Japanese Consular Service regarding voluntary restriction of the number of labourers sent to Canada.

The main point the Prime Minister of Canada made at the 1923 Imperial Conference was that some political and economic aspects of foreign policy were to a large extent an extension of domestic policy, and certain foreign policy issues were peculiar to Canada and required Canadian solutions. The good example he used was prohibition of the sale, manufacture and transportation of alcohol for consumption in the United States, a policy that had come into effect in January 1920 and had immense ramifications for trade and shipping. Some provinces in Canada had adopted forms of prohibition prior to the United States and these provincial policies had strong international ramifications, not least with the bordering United States.

The principle that Mackenzie King was now pushing for

was part of the evolution of policy instigated by Borden and now being presented as the right of each Dominion to control and direct its own foreign policy. Canada should control its own affairs, whether domestic or foreign. At the ninth meeting of the Imperial Conference of 1923, Mackenzie King clarified the position of Canada with regard to defence issues: 'So far as Canada is concerned, her attitude will continue to be in the future what it has been in the past, one namely, of hearty co-operation in matters of defence, having regard always to the fact that actual participation in war, the extent of participation and such like, must necessarily be matters which will have to be carefully considered and be decided by Parliament itself.' [33]

This principle, that Parliament would decide, is one to which Mackenzie King would return. On the nature of the British Empire, Mackenzie King reacted to the view expressed by the Australian Prime Minister, S M Bruce, that 'the British Empire is one and indivisible', as if it were the 'Godhead'.[34] Mackenzie King's response was strong: 'It is not true that in all particulars the Empire is indivisible; it is divisible, and very distinctly divisible. It is divisible geographically, racially, politically, and in a thousand ways, and we have to take account of all these divisions.' [35] Mackenzie King's position on the matter was an extension of the position developed by Sir Robert Borden, who had believed in the British Empire but believed Canada had autonomy over foreign policy matters and Canada would decide on the support it would give to the Empire.

7

Final Years: the Aftermath of the Peace Conferences

After Sir Robert Borden's return from the Washington conference in 1922, he largely retired from public life – he would have one last role as Canada's representative at the League of Nations in 1930 – but his continuing influence in the role of the Dominions in international affairs was seen in the drive towards a constitutional recognition of Canada's international position in the 1920s and 1930s. By 1924, when French-Canadian Senator Raoul Dandurand described Canada as 'a fire-proof house, far from inflammable materials',[1] Canada's control of its own foreign policy, very much through the previous work of Borden, had largely moved in advance of the position in international law. The recognition of Canada's foreign policy independence would be finally delivered in a declaration by Balfour in 1926 and the Statute of Westminster in 1931 that created the British Commonwealth of Nations.

The period would also see a series of international meetings attempting to deal with the more insidious issues that the Paris treaties left in their wake. The first of these was an inter-Allied conference in London in July and August 1924, which some saw as the most significant conference since the signing of the Treaty of Versailles. It was concerned with reparations, and the approval of the Dawes Plan, which required not only Allied consent but the approval of Germany in the amendment of provisions of the Treaty of Versailles. It was the Reparations Commission that in May 1921 determined the payments under articles of the Treaty of Versailles, with the exception of an agreement made in 1920 that the British Empire was to receive 22 per cent of the amount payable by Germany for reparations, 4.35 per cent of this payable to Canada, which was 0.957 per cent of the total reparations that Germany had to pay.[2]

French-Canadian Senator Raoul Dandurand (1861–1942), who in 1924 described Canada as 'a fire-proof house, far from inflammable materials', is probably most remembered for his views on Canada's isolationism. After establishing himself as a corporate lawyer in Quebec, he was appointed to the Senate at the young age of 37 and in 1905 became Speaker of the Senate. Prime Minister William Mackenzie King appointed Dandurand Minister of State in 1921 and he became a close ally of Mackenzie King. Dandurand represented Canada at the League of Nations for a number of years in the 1920s and late 1930s, specializing in issues relating to ethnic minorities. He became President of the Assembly in 1925.

The Dawes Committee under the American banker Charles Dawes had come up with a reparations plan for Germany and a reorganization of German banking. The attraction, beyond a more realistic scheme of payments, was the movement of the United States into European issues and its financial support for France. The Dawes Plan reduced the size of reparation payments for a period and helped to facilitate a loan from the United States. This allowed Germany to facilitate payments under the Dawes Plan, but it was with an American loan, a loan which financed German payments to European states which in turn repaid debts to the United States; this proved to be an unhealthy economic situation.

The payments under the Dawes plan from Germany to the Allied and Associated Powers became one billion gold marks in 1924–5, graduating to 2.5 billion gold marks in 1928–9, and was then related to a prosperity index. The share Canada would receive in reparations had to be negotiated against the costs of servicing a German loan, costs of various commissions and cost of armies of occupation; but Canada also became caught up in the economic consequences of these decisions and economic depression, and the Dawes Plan was replaced by the Young Plan (named after American businessman O D Young) of 1929 that led to a scaling down of reparation payments.

It was in Locarno in Switzerland in 1925 that some of the insecurities associated with the Paris treaties appeared to be overcome. The Locarno Pact – a series of treaties initialed at Locarno on 16 October 1925 and later signed in London – between the major European powers (Germany, Belgium, France, Great Britain and Italy) helped to produce strong political feelings throughout Europe that the Peace Conference of 1919 was being solidified into a workable proposition. The Treaty of Mutual Guarantee at the heart of the Locarno Pact led these major European powers to believe that peace might have been secured. The borders of Belgium and Germany, and France and Germany were accepted as inviolable and the demilitarisation of the Rhineland reinforced. The notion of guarantors made the Treaty of Mutual Guarantee novel and for many this encouraged optimism over western European security. Great Britain would be required to go to the aid of France or Germany in the event of an attack by one on the other. It was one of the guarantors of the peace. Italy and Belgium, although guarantors, were not seen as particularly significant players, but the agreement had the oddity of fascist Italy also being one of the guarantors of the peace. With Austen Chamberlain (British Foreign Secretary) in 1925, and Aristide Briand (French Foreign Minister) and Gustav Stresemann (German Minister of Foreign Affairs) in 1926 all receiving the Noble Peace Prize for their diplomatic efforts, a 'spirit of Locarno' was said to pervade European countries, and in particular Great Britain and France.[3]

The Locarno Pact also had its critics, particularly the arbitration treaties, which appeared to leave Eastern Europe, notably Czechoslovakia and Poland, open for future negotiations. Germany signed arbitration treaties with Poland and Czechoslovakia indicating that they would refer disputes to an arbitration tribunal. This always appeared less secure than the apparently firm agreement that applied to the western areas of Germany.

If Europe had a new stability, then it was also useful for Canada. Many of the agreements made at Locarno were applauded in Canada, particularly the inclusion of Article IX which excluded the Dominions and India from its obligations: 'The present Treaty shall impose no obligations upon any of the British dominions, or upon India, unless the Government of such dominion, or of India, signifies its acceptance thereof.'[4]

The main lesson of Locarno for Canada was that Britain was also looking to Europe for security and determining the policy as part of independent British foreign policy. There was little of direct interest to Canada. The ownership of Alsace Lorraine and the demilitarization of the Rhineland only interested Canada if the solutions maintained the peace. One historian has suggested that in accepting this, France,

Germany, Belgium and Italy 'openly recognized the peculiar nature of the British Commonwealth and gave the doctrine of "passive" and "active" responsibility a formal international endorsement which it had hitherto lacked.[5] Britain could make its own commitments to the European continent without the necessity of any collective decision-making involving the Dominions. In contrast, the lesson of Locarno for Borden was that the Dominions needed to take the initiative to prove their own national identity and not evade responsibility, which he believed was the policy of Mackenzie King.[6]

As a consequence of Locarno and the earlier Chanak Crisis, the British Foreign Office and the Dominions got around to prioritising their communications with one another. Locarno had raised the question of how independent the Dominions were in foreign policy affairs. The British view, as expressed by an assistant legal adviser to the Foreign Office, W E Beckett, was largely that the Dominions had not been consulted over Locarno, nor would they necessarily be consulted in the future as a consequence of the Treaty of Mutual Guarantee: '… any war involving Britain would probably involve the League of Nations, and would almost certainly be a war of self-defence. On both grounds the dominions were bound to be drawn in.'[7] For the Dominions, however, as Philip Wigley points out, although he expresses it rather strongly, 'it was equally certain that if ever Britain had to fulfil her Locarno responsibilities on the continent to maintain Franco-German equilibrium, she could count on little military support from her commonwealth partners'.[8]

The Imperial Conference of 1926 and the Balfour Declaration

The Imperial Conference of 1926 saw the British Foreign Office trying to compensate the Dominions for feelings of inadequacy that had been generated in the recent past. The British were prepared to engage in constitutional discussions. In 1926, South Africa, the Irish Free State and Canada had separate ideas and arguments for a defined equality of status. General James Barry Munnik Hertzog, Prime Minister of South Africa (Prime Minister for the long time of 1924 to 1939) and Desmond FitzGerald, Minister of External Affairs for the Irish Free State (Minister 1923–7; his son, Garrett, born 9 February 1926, would be a future Minister of External Affairs and Taoiseach of Eire), wanted a strong statement that defined their new independent constitutional status which they could take away from the conference. Mackenzie King, for Canada, had grown in political and international confidence by 1926 and was willing to work for a devolved status in British-Dominion relations that would be clearly in favour of the Dominions. All three wanted a definition of the legal status of the Dominions and how each Dominion and Britain related to one another.

Although it would appear that Mackenzie King was not thinking in quite such radical terms as the Irish and South Africans (who wanted a very strong statement on the independence of the individual Dominions on foreign policy issues), he also had personal reasons for taking an interest in the constitutional affairs of the British Empire. Canadian Governor General Lord Byng (Sir Julian Hedworth George Byng, Viscount Byng of Vimy) and Canadian Prime Minister Mackenzie King were parties in a dispute in 1925 and 1926. Mackenzie King had formed a minority Government in 1925,

Arthur James Balfour (1848–1930) was Prime Minister of Great Britain, 1902–5; Foreign Secretary, 1916–19; and was Chairman of the Inter-imperial Relations Committee at the Imperial Conference in 1926. He was also responsible for the Balfour Declaration of 1917, which endorsed the creation of a separate Jewish state in Palestine. Balfour was created Foreign Secretary in Lloyd George's Government in 1916 although he was not a member of the small War Cabinet. He was sympathetic to the Zionist cause for a Jewish homeland, and in a declaration on 2 November 1917 announced that the British Government favoured the establishment of a national home for Jews in Palestine, although he felt it should not prejudice the non-Jewish population there. After the Paris Peace Conference, to which he was a delegate and a signatory to the Treaty, he resigned as British Foreign Secretary. He maintained an interest in the League of Nations and led the British delegation in 1920–22. Balfour had contact with Borden over a number of years, and they were reacquainted at the Washington Naval Conference where Balfour and Borden were part of the British Empire delegation. A final great accomplishment was his chairing of the Inter-imperial Relations Committee at the Imperial Conference of 1926, the Balfour declaration on the independent status of the members of the Commonwealth and the resultant Statute of Westminster of 1931, produced after his death.

only to seek its dissolution prior to a motion of censure in the House of Commons in 1926. The Governor General denied Mackenzie King the request, but after Mackenzie King's resignation, accepted dissolution from Arthur Meighen. How much advice Byng took from Britain or should have taken is much disputed. Mackenzie King was re-elected in the General Election of 1926 as the 'constitutionally injured party'.[9] Should the Governor General represent the British Government in Canada and interfere in Canadian domestic affairs? This was the backdrop to Mackenzie King's contribution to the Imperial Conference. The Mackenzie King-Byng disagreement can be interpreted as the concluding motivation to an already deep-rooted wish for constitutional change with reference to the office of Governor General. The logical development of this awkward situation between the Prime Minister and Governor General was to question the perceived failed system of communications between the British Government and Canada. At the very least, the case managed to draw attention to the argument for constitutional restructuring; understood in Canada to mean an entirely sensible movement on the path to full equality between Britain and Canada.[10]

'[The Dominions and Britain were] ... autonomous communities within the British Empire, equal in status, in no way subordinate one to another in any respect of their domestic or external affairs, though united by a common allegiance to the Crown and freely associated as members of the British Commonwealth of Nations.'

BALFOUR DECLARATION, 1926

The Inter-imperial Relations Committee or Balfour Committee, as it was known after the chairman's name, had the task of coming up with new constitutional definitions that would suit all the participants of the Imperial Conference, but could also be declared publicly. The definition produced by Arthur Balfour, aided by Leopold Amery (Colonial Secretary and Dominions Secretary), provided that the Dominions and Britain were '... autonomous communities within the British Empire, equal in status, in no way subordinate one to another in any respect of their domestic or external affairs, though united by a common allegiance to the Crown and freely associated as members of the British Commonwealth of Nations.'[11] The outstanding nature of the declaration was the fact that Britain and the Dominions were now defined as 'equal in status'. Members of the British Commonwealth of Nations were there because they chose to be so.

The ideas of the Imperial Conference of 1926 were incorporated into the Statute of Westminster of 11 December 1931 which dealt with a number of legal ramifications of the new relationship between Britain and the Dominions. The requirement that the Dominions should not pass laws repugnant to English law was abolished as the Colonial Laws Validation Act was hereafter no longer to apply. It was also the case that an Act of the British Parliament could only apply to a Dominion if it had directly asked for this to be the case. Each of the Dominions acknowledged that it approved the provisions of the Statute of Westminster. A strong feeling existed within Government circles in Great Britain that this had not changed very much; rather, it brought the legal provisions of the constitution in line with what had become general practice.

One result of the changes, however, was that the British Government no longer communicated through the Governor General with the Canadian Government; instead, there was direct communication with the Secretary of State for External Affairs (a portfolio held by the Prime Minister). From 1928, Great Britain also provided a High Commissioner for Canada. Further, the Statute of Westminster meant the Dominions would not be committed to any foreign policy obligations without the approval of their own governments, something Canada believed to have been the case for some time.[12] Under the Treaty of Mutual Guarantee agreed at Locarno, the Dominions were not committed to guarantee the borders of Germany or France.

These changes, in fact, made Canada more passive rather than active in international affairs. The 1930s represented 'a period of consolidation that bordered on quiescence'; Canada did not push for further constitutional recognition but 'entered the ranks of the contented Dominions.'[13] Of course, the economic Great Depression contributed considerably to an insularity and isolationist tendency in Canada, as did the political and security uncertainties in Europe and the Far East.

Borden's last years

During the last 15 years of his life, Borden was a keen advocate of the League of Nations, having been made president of the League of Nations Society in Canada. This led him to give speeches on behalf of the society and provide help in organizing branches throughout Canada. Borden also chaired the first meeting of the Canadian Institute of International Affairs. Although it is now situated at the University of Toronto, its first executive meeting was held at Robert Borden's home, Glensmere, in Ottawa. These strong educational interests continued as he became Chancellor of Queen's University, Ontario from 1924 to 1930 (he had held a similar office at McGill University, Quebec 1918–20) and also became president of the Canadian Historical Association.[14]

Though now an old man, Borden was no less vigorous in mind and was still recognised as one of Canada's elder statesman. It appeared very fitting then that Borden, despite being 76 years old, led the Canadian delegation to the League of Nations in 1930 as a replacement for Senator Dandurand. There was a strong rumour he was coming to Europe to be the High Commissioner for Canada in London, and to his irritation it was this question that greeted him on his arrival at Southampton as he disembarked from the Canadian Pacific liner *Empress of Scotland*. Borden was to travel on to Paris and then Geneva where he represented Canada on the Council of the League of Nations until the country's membership in the Council expired in that year. As Borden explained to the press, *With some hesitation I acceded to the request of the Canadian Prime Minister that I should undertake the duty of representing Canada during the remaining term of her membership in the Council of the League of Nations. He also requested that I should act as chief of the Canadian Delegation to the Assembly of the League. It had been my firm determination to accept no further official duty; but as the questions to arise in both the Council and the Assembly are of the highest importance, and as I had a leading part in the effort which gave to the Dominions the right of nomination and election to the Council, I finally consented to accept the task.*[15]

After returning from Geneva, Borden continued to play golf and work in his office. As late as 1933 he started his *Letters to Limbo* (only published in 1971) to collect his thoughts on issues of the day. Borden wrote letters to an imaginary newspaper, the *Limbo Recorder and Guardian*; he wrote 20 letters in 1933 and wrote another 55 from 1934 to 1937. Much of his time was spent on his *Memoirs* (published in two volumes in 1938), with his friends and in his garden. However, he travelled to France to participate in the unveiling of the Vimy War Memorial in July 1936. He was overlooked in terms of the speeches, but found the visit to war graves exceedingly moving.

In June 1937, Sir Robert Laird Borden died in Ottawa at the age of 82. There was no lying in state. The state funeral took place at All Saints' Church in Ottawa, after a small family service at Glensmere. From Glensmere a funeral procession led by the Royal Canadian Mounted Police and the band of the Governor General's Foot Guards moved to All Saints' Church and passed First World War veterans lining the route. Formal representatives of the King and the Government of

Canada were represented at the funeral. The honorary pall bearers were surviving members of his Cabinet and joined 400 people in the church, reflecting the breadth of organisations to which Borden had belonged. He was buried at Beechwood Cemetery in Ottawa with a simple tombstone that excluded the title Sir, which had been his wish. His wife, Laura, who died in 1940, is buried next to him. Borden's obituary in *The Times* of London described him as the 'grand *seigneur* of the Canadian political world' and highlighted his 'patience and sagacity'.[16] Former Prime Minister Arthur Meighen stated, 'This country had a strong steady leader in the dark days of the War, and the British Government had a valued counsellor on whom Ministers depended. No other Canadian ever bore so crushing a burden.'[17]

8

Peace and War: Canada's Place in World Affairs

One of the legacies of Borden's attitudes towards the First World War was the approach taken by Prime Minister Mackenzie King at the start of the Second World War. Borden's war aims had been to emphasise the defence of civilisation and humanity and not just go to war because Britain was at war. Mackenzie King would take an even stronger line than Borden and independently declare war on Germany. However the tone and approach by both Prime Ministers was very similar. As Borden said, and Mackenzie King might easily have done, *the chief insignia of a civilized nation are orderly government and respect for the law.*[1]

Borden expected a strong autonomous Canada to function within the British Commonwealth: *It is instructive and satisfactory to observe how strong a spirit of Canadianism animates those of our people who were born in the British Isles, and to whom the unity of the Empire is a vital consideration. The assumption of equal nationhood carries with it grave responsibilities. There is no alternative except complete independence, whereof the responsibilities will assuredly be not less onerous.*[2] Although Borden worked for Canada having a much greater say within the British Empire and Dominions relationship, he still expected co-operation and understanding to be the bedrock of that relationship, and he expected equality within the Commonwealth.

Borden had always been concerned about the success of the Paris Peace Conference in creating a workable peace in Europe and beyond, and as early as 1921 he was worried about the application of the principle of national self-determination. *The creation or recognition of numerous small states, whose populations are wholly untrained in self-government, can hardly assist in preventing war. That every race should clothe itself in the garment of self-determination is in theory wholly unwise and in practice wholly unworkable.*[3] Intriguingly, a revisionist power like Germany could also make its own claim to implement national self-determination for German-speaking people. Yet, the League of Nations existed to protect the sovereignty of nation-states against the unbridled aggression of revisionist powers. It was the Manchurian Incident in 1931 that first tested these powers.

The Japanese invasion of Manchuria in China in the 1930s was part of an attempt by Japan to secure economic resources for itself as an industrial power and create an empire that Japanese militaristic cliques longed for. European powers of the League of Nations were not in a sufficiently satisfactory military or economic position to be able to combat them. For Canada, the Manchurian Incident did not underline the worries Canada harboured about Article X since the League of Nations did not intervene, but only set up the Lytton Commission to investigate the outbreak of the crisis. Canada supported its conclusions and rejected recognition of the Japanese puppet state of Manchukuo. As a result, Japan withdrew from the League of Nations, which did not bode well for peaceful settlements. The occasion largely managed to show that military action by the League of Nations in the Far East was extremely unlikely without the involvement of the United States. It also demonstrated the weaknesses of an organisation that had not been devised on the basis that its significant members would abuse it.

Failures associated with the League of Nations over the Manchurian Crisis suggested that the organisation might well be tested again by powers wishing to revise the Paris settlements. The crisis of 1935 when Italy invaded Abyssinia brought unified criticism from the Commonwealth. Canada and the other Commonwealth countries approved the declaration of the League of Nations, which blamed Italy as the aggressor, but the Canadian Government had reservations about implementing sanctions, and they were not alone in this.

The Canadian delegation under Conservative politician George Howard Ferguson (Canadian High Commissioner to London since December 1930) and Walter A Riddell (Canadian Advisory Officer at the League of Nations, 1925–37; he had also worked at the International Labour Organisation in Geneva from 1920–5) was an advocate of collective security. Riddell, however, became over-enthusiastic about sanctions against Italy and, misinterpreting instructions from Ottawa or acting without clear instructions, supported the view that restrictions should be put on not only arms shipments but coal, oil, iron and steel. This had not been the intention of the Canadian Government in Ottawa, although Prime Minister Richard Bennet's leadership (Conservative Prime Minister, 7 August 1930–23 October 1935), or rather lack of it, has been much criticised: 'In Rome these sanctions were branded as "the Canadian proposals".'[4] The Canadian Government managed to disassociate itself from Riddell's endorsement of sanctions against Italy and endeavoured to operate a more coherent and cautious policy in the future. Bennett's ultimate view was to see Italy labelled the aggressor and for once he rather strongly expressed the point: 'No doubt we signed the Covenant; no doubt of Italy's guilt; we must take the consequences.'[5]

International crises do not always come at the right time for democracies and Italy's invasion of Abyssinia in October 1935 was in the background during the Canadian general election that year. The result saw Bennett removed from office and the reinstatement of the Liberal Party with Mackenzie King as Prime Minister. Mackenzie King did not want to declare war over Abyssinia: he was concerned about Roman Catholic support in Canada (notably in Quebec) and had no desire to fight a Catholic Italy and major power of the League of Nations, nor to upset the United States by instituting trade embargoes since trade was such an important election issue. Despite Mackenzie King's best statements to the contrary, the proposal of oil sanctions continued to be associated with Canada within the League of Nations. The United States' opposition to oil sanctions, however, exposed the real ineffectiveness of the League of Nations. It was not the League of Nations' finest hour, or that of Canada, which merely added to the confusion surrounding what should be done about Italy. All sanctions would eventually be dropped by the League, and the status quo of Italian control of the invaded territories accepted.

On 5 May 1936, in one of his *Letters to Limbo*, Sir Robert Borden lamented the Italian invasion of Abyssinia and the failure of the League of Nations. It was a letter that it must have pained him to write: *As first Japan, then Germany and now Italy have flouted and defied the League of Nations; it is apparent that its usefulness has reached the vanishing point.*[6] A European war appeared on the horizon and Borden was both pessimistic and sad.

The implication of the failure of the League of Nations over Manchuria and Abyssinia was to put an emphasis both on the significance of Commonwealth defence and on appeasement as an effective diplomatic approach. Many post-Versailles Canadians found the peace treaties vindictive in their territorial arrangements, and Canada did not show any strong opposition to Hitler's re-militarisation of the Rhineland. Canada was not alone in this: in Britain, too, there was some sympathy for Germany's position.

In this turmoil of fear and hatred, of distrust, envy, jealousy and suspicion, of antagonistic nationalism, of supreme reliance on sheer force and violence, one may wonder whether what we call our civilization is destined or indeed has the right to survive.

ROBERT BORDEN, *LETTERS TO LIMBO*, 5 MAY 1936

The practical implication of Borden's push for redefined Dominion status was that Great Britain now could not rely on the Dominions in an international conflict. Canada did not wish to show a willingness to be involved in war. The ability to make its own foreign policy meant Canada could disassociate itself from European problems and had the choice as to whether or not to commit itself to military action. Appeasement suited Canada's acceptance of a form of isolationism, and since Great Britain could not assume the support of Commonwealth nations, then appeasement was equally appropriate for the 'mother country'. The Imperial Conference of 1937 was thus somewhat dominated by the failure of the League of Nations and the acceptance of appeasement.

The Czechoslovakian crisis of 1938 allowed appeasement to be pushed a step further as the Commonwealth nations had to be considered by the British Government, and this helped to produce a policy of appeasement towards Adolf Hitler's plans for the annexation of the German-speaking areas of Czechoslovakia. This is not to say that Neville Chamberlain adopted the policy because of the views of Mackenzie King; it is more the case that they shared similar attitudes towards Germany and preserving the peace. At the time of the annexation of the rest of Czechoslovakia in March 1939, Mackenzie King spoke to the Canadian House of Commons: 'If there were a prospect of an aggressor launching an attack on Britain, with bombers raining death on London, I have no doubt what the decision of the Canadian people and parliament would be. We would regard it as an act of aggression, menacing freedom in all parts of the British Commonwealth.'[7] His statement reflected the change in constitutional status: a British Commonwealth as opposed to a British Empire and Dominions, and the sovereignty of the Canadian Parliament. While the result would be much the same, Canada could clearly now choose to stand at Britain's side.

The Second World War

After the failure of appeasement and Germany's blatant attack on Poland on 1 September 1939, the Commonwealth members of Canada, Australia, South Africa and New Zealand decided to become directly involved in the war. Eire remained neutral throughout. Each of the Dominion states decided on its own participation independently. Although Australia and New Zealand were not committed to war by the British declaration, they considered themselves committed. Mackenzie King would take the time to make it clear that Canada was entering the war as an independent nation and as a result of an independent decision. He evoked his phrase of 'Parliament would decide', and after a Parliamentary debate, Canada declared war just seven days after Britain on 10 September.

Unlike the First World War, there was no gleeful rush to arms in Canada. The memories of the experiences and the losses in the First World War and the deprivations of the Depression had made sure that a more plaintive approach would be undertaken by the public, press and politicians. It does not appear overstated for Norman Hillmer and Jack Granatstein to point out rather ruefully, 'It was almost as if Sir Robert Borden's valiant efforts to secure Canada a voice in decisions a quarter-century before had never occurred; it was almost as if King's own struggle for autonomy had been blown away by the first shots of World War II.'[8] The old adage that the first casualty of war is democracy seems particularly applicable to the Second World War.

Centralised decision-making was required for Great Britain itself, as civil defence and military measures had to be put into place; and to no-one's surprise, the Allied war effort for the Commonwealth was coordinated from London. It must have been galling to the Commonwealth countries to see Great Britain being described as 'standing alone' after the collapse of France (France signed an armistice on 22 June 1940). Although this view served British propaganda in its efforts to encourage the United States out of its 'non-belligerency', Canada's contribution to the war was being 'ignored' more than in the First World War. There would be no equivalent to the Imperial War Cabinet of the First World War and with Winston Churchill as Prime Minister from May 1940 and the United States entering the war in December 1941, the Anglo-American approach to the war dominated. With the emergence of the Big Three Alliance, with the Soviet Union accepted temporarily into the bosom of Western diplomacy, further reasons for Commonwealth states to be marginalised developed. While Mackenzie King accepted his position on the periphery of wartime military and diplomatic organisation, he worked hard to see the military contribution of Canada acknowledged.

In the security of Ottawa, the Canadian Department of External Affairs could promote new policies for Canada, whilst working on practical matters to win the war. Canada also had a lot of good civil service minds to think about what Canada would gain from the war. A legacy of the Borden years and the professionalism of the small Department of External Affairs was to see a number of excellent university graduates wanting to work for Canada and represent Canada abroad. Canada's 'best and brightest' included Lester B Pearson, Escott Reid, Dana Wilgress, Norman Robertson and Hume Wrong.

Functional Representation and Canada as a Middle Power

The development of a new international order during and after the Second World War encouraged Canada to support functional representation and position itself as a Middle Power. In practical terms, this meant it envisaged a shared responsibility in international organisations, with the importance of the contributions that members made to international organisations being rewarded with responsibility and authority within them. In the development of its foreign policy Canada would draw on its experiences at the Paris

Peace Conferences, representation in the League of Nations and in particular a functionalist organisation like the International Labour Organisation.

Functionalism was promoted by Lester Bowles Pearson (Minister-Counsellor, Legation and subsequently Embassy in the United States, 1942–45) and Hume Wrong (Assistant Under-Secretary of State for External Affairs, 1942–44) as an academic answer to Canada's demands for a significant post-Second World War status. They believed Canada could contribute to social, economic and humanitarian international organizations and would subsequently be compensated with significant roles within them.[9] For Canada, membership of international organisations, from the Imperial and Paris Peace Conferences to the new post-Second World War international organisations such as League successor the United Nations, was part of the process whereby the country moved from being an unofficial 'colony' to a nation.

The functionalist doctrine was to prove less durable than the notion of Canada being a Middle Power. Canada brought rationality towards peacekeeping because Canadian diplomats were not hindered by Great Power political and military status. And its status as a Middle Power, a depiction it became very comfortable with, also differentiated it from both Great Britain and the United States.

The big move from the time of Borden was that Canadian foreign policy was no longer wedded to the British Empire. There no longer needed to be a common foreign policy for Great Britain, Empire and Commonwealth; Canada was not in favour of a single foreign policy for the Commonwealth. Whereas Borden had expected this, in May 1944 Prime Minister Winston Churchill's suggestions for a British Commonwealth and Empire representation in post-war international organisations was summarily rejected by Mackenzie King. Canada was aware that the Commonwealth gave it a new identity, and would not turn the clock back to before the First World War.

As British power in international politics declined in the years that followed the Second World War, Canada found that the Commonwealth had a less rigid framework to operate in, which suited the country and its citizens, enabling them to gain a new confidence in their own sense of national identity. 'Canadian nationalists,' stated Canadian diplomat and scholar John Holmes, 'no longer afraid the British were restricting their freedom, saw in the Commonwealth a counterforce to the threat of Canadian independence'.[10]

From Borden to Mackenzie King, Canada had worked hard on the idea of independent foreign policy decision-making, and although Borden was happy to work with the British Empire and Mackenzie King with Great Britain, the driving force for both was independent representation. 'If Borden's name is to be blazoned on the roll of Canada's great Prime Ministers,' Charles Stacey wrote of the mostly reserved Nova Scotian, 'it is because of what he did to achieve a new position for her in the Empire and the world.'[11]

Conclusion

Sir Robert Borden, a rather private and shy man, was a strange choice for Prime Minister of Canada, and it is doubly strange for him to have been the one to lead Canada through an international war. His legal background, business interests, fishing and golf hardly prepared him for his work in the First World War. Yet, he had the fortitude and bravery to oversee difficult decisions and had a clear sense of purpose throughout the war and in building the peace. To his credit, and despite hostility over the issue of conscription, Borden prudently avoided party political speeches during the First World War. He is remembered as one of the more significant figures in Canadian history and politics.

Borden's commitment to international issues was evident through his adult life. He could hardly avoid the issue of naval defence in Opposition or as Prime Minister. The First World War made him a war leader, but involvement in the Imperial War Cabinet, the Paris Peace Conference, the League of Nations and the Washington Naval Disarmament Conference made him a memorable international statesman.

Only two years after the Paris Peace Conference, Borden reported in a lecture to the University of Toronto, *Of those who took part in the Peace Conference at Paris some at least returned to this continent with a sense of depression. The fierce antagonisms, the ancient hatreds, and the bitter jealousies of European nationals there assembled were not inspiring.* Borden's worries about the difficulties between ethnic groups and the application of the principle of national self-determination in Europe were to prove prophetic as racial issues played an enormous role in the descent towards the Second World War.

Sir Robert Borden's own conclusion about the League of Nations in May 1936, when he was nearly 82, was that it had failed, but that this might have been avoided. *And the League need not have failed. Assuredly it would not have failed if the rulers of United States had possessed wisdom at all comparable to that country's influence and power. It has been well said that in 1919, United States abdicated the moral leadership of the world.*[1] As a lover of history, Borden was aware of speculation and counter-factual arguments, but the literary device of *Letters to Limbo* allowed him to speculate as much as he liked. *With [the] United States leading and dominating the League, neither Japan, nor Germany, nor Italy would have dared pursue the course they have taken. In the absence of that leadership, these three nations have been enabled to uphold force as the vital consideration, its dominance as the highest political wisdom, its use as the ultimate resort.*[2]

John English has described Borden as 'author of disunity yet creator of independence'.[3] There was indeed much disunity during Borden's Premiership: acrimonious naval debates, the conscription crisis, some dictatorial wartime legislation, conflict over the creation of a Unionist Government, war casualties, language issues and economic problems. Yet, as history books record, Borden was the only Allied leader to last through the war from start to finish. He enhanced democratic rights for women, produced a successful coalition government, and brought Canada to the peace table and ultimately to independent international legal status. It would be surprising if political leadership of the length of Borden's was not without considerable highs and lows or triumph and disaster.

No doubt, Sir Robert Borden is remembered as being Canada's Prime Minister during the First World War and, more controversially, for introducing conscription. It is also the case that Borden is remembered fondly for championing autonomy for Canadian foreign policy, Dominion representation in international conferences and providing more coherence to Imperial foreign policy. His work in the Imperial War Cabinet, representing Canada at the Paris Peace Conference and on the British Empire delegation in Paris gave him a strong sense of responsibility and maturity as a statesman. The model of the British Empire delegation later served well for the Washington Naval Disarmament Conference delegation to which Borden was also appointed. It was these international conferences of the First World War and the Statute of Westminster in 1931 that defined Canada's place in world affairs. For this international work alone, Borden should be remembered as a crucial figure in Canadian history.

Borden was not an orator like Sir Wilfrid Laurier or David Lloyd George, and his speeches are not memorable. More arguably, he does not appear to have been an original thinker, although he was clearly well read. He had no great eccentricities, but believed in old-fashioned public service and duty. Canada and Borden appeared to be in tandem, not revolutionary, not radical, but capable of prompting change at the appropriate time and at a pace that suited them both.

Borden's concluding words to his *Memoirs* as he accepted retirement sound modest, even pessimistic: *Democracy is always ungrateful, forgetful and neglectful.*[4] This was, however, not to be the case with Sir Robert Borden.

Notes

Preface

1. B Hutchison, *Mr Prime Minister, 1867–1964* (Harcourt, Brace & World, Inc, New York: 1965) p 149.
2. J English, 'Political leadership in the First World War' in D MacKenzie, *Canada and the First World War: Essays in Honour of Robert Craig Brown* (University of Toronto Press, Toronto: 2005) p 77; hereafter English in MacKenzie.
3. C P Stacey, *Canada and the Age of Conflict: A History of Canadian External Policies, Vol 1: 1867–1921* (The Macmillan Company of Canada Ltd, Toronto: 1977) p 256; hereafter Stacey.
4. See in particular the *Oxford Dictionary of National Biography*, www.oxforddnb.com, and the *Dictionary of Canadian Biography*, www.biographi.ca.
5. www.theglobeandmail.com.
6. M MacMillan, 'Canada and the Peace Settlements', in MacKenzie, p 381; hereafter MacMillan in MacKenzie. Professor Margaret MacMillan is the great-granddaughter of David Lloyd George.

7. R Veatch, *Canada and the League of Nations* (University of Toronto Press, Toronto: 1975) p 20; hereafter Veatch.

1: The Coming of Age of Canada

1. R L Borden, *Canadian Constitutional Studies: The Marfleet Lectures, University of Toronto, October 1921* (Oxford University Press, London: 1922) footnote 25, p 13; hereafter Borden, *Canadian Constitutional Studies.*
2. J D B Miller, *Britain and the Old Dominions* (Chatto & Windus, London: 1966) pp 15–6.
3. A Siegfried, *Canada: an International Power* (Arno Press, New York: 1972) p 74.
4. English in MacKenzie, p 81.
5. L C Clark (ed), *Documents on Canadian External Relations*, Vol 3, 1919–1925 (Information Canada, Ottawa: 1970) p 524; hereafter *DCER*.
6. H Borden (ed), *Robert Laird Borden: His Memoirs*, Vol 1 (The Macmillan Company of Canada Ltd, Toronto: 1938) pp 357–8; hereafter Borden, *Memoirs*.
7. J L Granatstein, *Towards a New World: Readings in the History of Canadian Foreign Policy* (Copp Clark Pitman, Toronto: 1992) p 8; hereafter Granatstein, *Towards a New World.*
8. Granatstein, *Towards a New World*, p 8.
9. J Eayrs, *In Defence of Canada, From the Great War to the Great Depression* (University of Toronto Press, Toronto: 1967) p 3; hereafter Eayrs.
10. Eayrs, pp 3–4.

11. R M Dawson (ed), *The Development of Dominion Status, 1900–1936* (Frank Cass & Co, London: 1965) p 4; hereafter Dawson.
12. D Lloyd George, *Memoirs of the Peace Conference*, Vol 1 (Yale University Press, New Haven: 1939) p 368.
13. *DCER*, Vol 3, 1919–1925, p 255.
14. L Oppenheim, *International Law: A Treatise, Vol 1, Peace* (8th edition; Longmans, Green, London: 1955), section 94a in Borden, *Canadian Constitutional Studies,* footnote 25, p 161.
15. Oppenheim, *International Law,* section 94b; in Borden, *Canadian Constitutional Studies*, pp 161–2.
16. W D McIntyre, *The Commonwealth of Nations: Origins and Impact, 1869–1971* (University of Minnesota Press, Minneapolis: 1977) p 5; hereafter McIntyre.
17. McIntyre, p 5.
18. Borden, *Canadian Constitutional Studies*, p 11.
19. R A MacKay (ed), *DCER*, *Vol 2, The Paris Peace Conference of 1919* (Queen's Printer, Ottawa: 1969) p ix.
20. See in particular Veatch.
21. Veatch, p 22.
22. Veatch, p 23.

2: Development of a Future Leader

1. Borden, *Memoirs,* Vol 1, p 4.
2. J L Granatstein, *The Ottawa Men: The Civil Service Mandarins, 1935–1957* (Oxford University Press, Toronto: 1982) p 6.
3. Borden, *Memoirs,* Vol 1, p 4.

4. R C Brown, *Robert Laird Borden: A Biography*, Vol 1 (The Macmillan Company of Canada Ltd, Toronto: 1975), p 5; hereafter Brown, *Borden*, Vol 1.
5. Borden, *Memoirs*, Vol 1, p 5.
6. Brown, *Borden*, Vol 1, p 9.
7. Borden, *Memoirs,* Vol 1, p 14.
8. Brown, *Borden*, Vol 1, p 17.
9. Borden, Memoirs, Vol 1, p 15.
10. K Saunders, *Robert Borden* (Fitzhenry & Whiteside Limited, Ontario: 1978) p 6; hereafter Saunders.
11. Brown, *Borden*, Vol 1, p 24.
12. Borden, *Memoirs*, Vol 1, p 29.
13. Borden, *Memoirs,* Vol 1, p 28.
14. Borden, *Memoirs*, Vol 1, pp 37–41.
15. Borden, *Memoirs*, Vol 1, p 50.
16. Dawson, pp 135–6.
17. R C Brown on 'Borden, Sir Robert Laird' in *Dictionary of Canadian Biography*, www.biographi.ca.
18. Borden to Charles Hibbert Tupper, in Brown, *Borden*, Vol 1, p 48.
19. Brown, *Borden,* Vol 1, p 48.
20. Borden, *Memoirs,* Vol 1, p 74.
21. Borden, *Memoirs,* Vol 1, p 74.
22. Brown, *Borden,* Vol 1, p 53.
23. Brown, *Borden,* Vol 1, p 150.

3: Prime Minister Robert Borden

1. Stacey, p 153.
2. Borden, *Memoirs,* Vol 1, p 268.
3. Borden, *Memoirs*, Vol 1, p 276.
4. Borden, *Memoirs*, Vol 1, p 273.

5. N Hillmer and J L Granatstein, *Empire to Umpire* (Copp Clark Longman Ltd, Toronto: 1994) p 30, hereafter Hillmer and Granatstein.
6. R C Brown on 'Borden, Sir Robert Laird', in *Dictionary of Canadian Biography*, www.biographi.ca
7. Saunders, p 28.
8. Brown, *Borden*, Vol 1, p 231.
9. R C Brown, 'Sir Robert Borden, The Great War, and Anglo-Canadian Relations', in Granatstein, *Towards a New World*, p 30. Eayrs comments from *In Defence of Canada*, p 23, are cited by F H Soward, 'The Department of External Affairs and Canadian Autonomy, 1899–1939', Booklet No 7 (The Canadian Historical Association, Ottawa: 1972; reprint of 1956) p 10; hereafter Soward.
10. Hillmer and Granatstein, p 54.
11. Saunders, p 31.
12. Borden, *Memoirs*, Vol 1, p 451.
13. Borden, *Memoirs*, Vol 1, p 453.
14. Stacey, *Canada and the Age of Conflict*, p 158.
15. Saunders, p 31.
16. Borden, *Memoirs*, Vol 1, p 428.
17. Saunders, p 33.
18. Stacey, p 160.
19. Brown, 'Borden, Sir Robert Laird', *Dictionary of Canadian Biography*, www.biographi.ca.

4: Rough Road to Versailles: the First World War and the Planning for Peace

1. Borden, *Memoirs*, Vol 1, p 456.
2. Borden, *Memoirs*, Vol 1, p 461.

3. Brown, *Robert Laird Borden: A Biography*, Vol 2 (The Macmillan Company of Canada Ltd, Toronto: 1980) p 10; hereafter Brown, *Borden*, Vol 2.
4. Stacey, p 176.
5. Dawson, p 17.
6. Brown, 'Sir Robert Borden, The Great War, and Anglo-Canadian Relations', in Granatstein, *Towards a New World*, p 30.
7. Brown, *Borden,* Vol 2, p 69.
8. Saunders, p 37.
9. *The Times*, 29 June 1915, p 7.
10. Saunders, p 37.
11. N Mansergh, *The Commonwealth Experience* (Weidenfeld and Nicolson, London: 1969) p 170.
12. *DCER*, Vol 1, 1909–1918 (Queen's Printer, Ottawa: 1967) p 104.
13. *DCER*, Vol 1, 1909–1918, p 104.
14. *DCER*, Vol 1, 1909–1918, p 104.
15. Brown, 'Sir Robert Borden, The Great War, and Anglo-Canadian Relations,' in Granatstein, *Towards a New World*, p 36.
16. Borden's Diary, 24 August 1915, cited in Brown, *Borden,* Vol 2, p 31.
17. G L Cook, 'Sir Robert Borden, Lloyd George and British Military Policy, 1917–1918', *The Historical Journal*, Vol XIV, No 2 (June 1971) p 371.
18. Saunders, p 41.
19. Brown, *Borden,* Vol 2, p 70.
20. Lloyd George, *Memoirs of the Peace Conference*, p 53.
21. P G Wigley, *Canada and the Transition to Commonwealth: British-Canadian Relations 1917–1926*

(Cambridge University Press, Cambridge: 1977) p 29; hereafter Wigley.
22. R L Borden and J C Smuts, *The Empire and the War: The Voice of the Dominions* (The Empire Parliamentary Association, London: 1917) p 12.
23. Dawson, p 23.
24. Brown, *Borden,* Vol 2, p 75.
25. Lloyd George, *Memoirs of the Peace Conference,* p.70.
26. Brown, *Borden,* Vol 2, p 81.
27. Brown, *Borden,* Vol 2, p 81.
28. Dawson, pp 25–6.
29. Wigley, p 42.
30. Brown, *Borden,* Vol 2, p 83.
31. Brown, *Borden,* Vol 2, p 84.
32. Brown, *Borden,* Vol 2, p 100.
33. Saunders, pp 47–8.
34. Saunders, p 49.
35. Brown 'Sir Robert Borden, The Great War, and Anglo-Canadian Relations', in Granatstein, *Towards a New World*, p 33.
36. English in MacKenzie, p 77.
37. Wigley, p 63.
38. Brown, *Borden,* Vol 2, p 142.
39. *DCER*, Vol 3, 1919–1925, p 58.
40. *DCER*, Vol 3, 1919–1925, pp 66–7.
41. Stacey, p 241.
42. Saunders, p 52.
43. *The Times*, 14 November 1918, p 5.
44. Saunders, p 52.
45. Soward, p 10.
46. Brown, *Borden,* Vol 2, p 77.
47. Hillmer and Granatstein, p 59.

5: Anglo-Canadian relations at Versailles

1. Stacey, p 238.
2. White to Borden, 4 December 1918, Lloyd George Papers, House of Lords Record Office, F/5/2/29, hereafter LGP.
3. Brown, *Borden*, Vol 1, p 150.
4. *DCER*, Vol 2, 1919, p 8.
5. *DCER*, Vol 2, 1919, p 71.
6. *DCER*, Vol 2, 1919, p 8.
7. *DCER*, Vol 2, 1919, p 88.
8. Stacey, p 244.
9. Stacey, p 245.
10. Wigley, p 78.
11. Stacey, p 245.
12. *DCER*, Vol 2, 1919, p 23.
13. www.oxforddnb.com/public/themes and LGP, F/5/3/34.
14. A Sharp, *David Lloyd George: Great Britain* (Haus Publishing, London: 2008) p 58.
15. Borden, *Memoirs*, Vol 2, p 902.
16. LGP, F/5/3/1. Also mentioned in M L Dockrill and Z Steiner, 'The Foreign Office at the Paris Peace Conference in 1919', *International History Review*, Vol 11, No 1 (1980), p 56.
17. Borden, *Memoirs*, Vol 2, p 903.
18. Brown, *Borden*, p 153.
19. Borden, *Memoirs*, Vol 2, p 903.
20. Borden, *Memoirs*, Vol 2, p 908.
21. National Archives of Canada, R L Borden, Fonds, Notes on Paris Peace Conference, hereafter NAC, Borden, Microfilm C-44449, p 173306; *DCER* , Vol 2, 1919, p 189.

22. NAC, Borden, Microfilm C-44449, p 173306; *DCER*, Vol 2, 1919, p 189.
23. NAC, Borden, Microfilm C-44449, p 173306; *DCER*, Vol 2, 1919, p 189.
24. Wigley, p 78.
25. Wigley, p 80.
26. M MacMillan, *Peacemakers: The Paris Peace Conference of 1919 and Its Attempt to End War* (John Murray, London: 2001) p 83.
27. Wigley, p 84.
28. *DCER*, Vol 2, 1919, p 208.
29. 8 February 1919, LGP, No 4, Folder 3, Box 38, F/5/3/5.
30. MacMillan in MacKenzie, p 383.
31. 27 March 1919, LGP, No 21, Folder 3, Box 38, F/5/3/27.
32. NAC, Borden, Microfilm C-4449, p 173423.
33. MacMillan in MacKenzie, p 398.
34. LGP, F/5/3/27.
35. 1 April 1919, LGP, No 22, Folder 3, Box 38, F/5/3/30.
36. MacMillan in MacKenzie, p 399.
37. MacMillan in MacKenzie, p 390.
38. Borden to Lloyd George, 29 April 1919, *DCER*, Vol 2, 1919, p 136.
39. Borden, *Memoirs*, Vol. 2, p 927.
40. Paris, 2 April 1919, *DCER*, Vol 2, 1919, p 104.
41. Borden, *Memoirs*, Vol 2, p 927.
42. LGP, F/5/3/32; *DCER*, Vol 2, 1919, pp 116–7.
43. LGP, F/5/3/32; *DCER*, Vol 2, 1919, pp 116–7.
44. NAC, Borden, Microfilm C-4449, p 173304.
45. 6 May 1919, Veatch, p 6.
46. Saunders, p 54.
47. Veatch, p 72.
48. *DCER*, Vol 2, 1919, p 58.

49. Eayrs, p 7.
50. NAC, Borden, Microfilm C-4449, pp 173241–173257.
51. NAC, Borden, Microfilm C-4449, p 173247.
52. NAC, Borden, Microfilm C-4449, p 173247.
53. Eayrs, p 8.
54. H W V Temperley (ed), *A History of the Peace Conference of Paris*, Vol VI (Oxford University Press, London: 1969) p 350.
55. Borden, *Memoirs*, Vol 2, p 962.
56. Borden, *Memoirs*, Vol 2, p 963.
57. Borden, *Memoirs*, Vol 2, p 963.
58. Borden, *Memoirs*, Vol 2, p 976.
59. LGP, F/5/3/34.
60. *DCER*, Vol 2, 1919, p 109.
61. Borden, *Canadian Constitutional Studies,* p 120.
62. Borden to Lloyd George, 13 May 1919, LGP F/5/3/61.
63. Wigley, p 93.
64. Wigley, p 94.
65. Stacey, pp 257–8.
66. Stacey, p 289.
67. Stacey, p 290.
68. Stacey, p 294.
69. Soward, p 10.
70. Stacey, p 250.
71. Stacey, p 241.
72. D Lloyd George, *War Memoirs,* Vol IV (Odhams, London: 1934) p 1743; Brown, *Borden,* Vol 2, pp 77–8.

6: The Early Post-war Years

1. MacMillan in MacKenzie, p 401.
2. Borden, *Memoirs*, Vol 2, p 913.

3. Canadian Governor General to Chargé d'Affaires in United States, from Ottawa, 7 July 1919, *DCER*, Vol 3, 1919–1925, p 4.
4. NAC, Sir Robert L Borden, OC series, Vol 119, Microfilm C-4345, p 65814.
5. Veatch, p 77.
6. Veatch, p 88.
7. Veatch, p 88.
8. *DCER*, Vol 3, 1919–1925, p 486.
9. Wigley, p 145.
10. Wigley, p 148.
11. *New York Evening Post*, 18 November 1921; NAC, Borden, Microfilm C-4345, p 65729.
12. *DCER*, Vol 3, 1919–1925, p 506.
13. Stacey, p 351.
14. *DCER*, Vol 3, 1919–1925, p 491.
15. *DCER*, Vol 3, 1919–1925, p 505.
16. Memorandum from Mackenzie King to Sir Robert Borden, 28 January 1922, *DCER*, Vol 3, 1919–1925, p 510.
17. Borden to Mackenzie King, from Washington, 31 January 1922, *DCER*, Vol 3, 1919–1925, p 511.
18. Telegram, Borden to Mackenzie King, 2 February 1922, *DCER*, Vol 3, 1919–1925, p 513.
19. NAC, Borden, Microfilm C-4345, p 65836A.
20. NAC, Borden, Microfilm C-4345, p 65836B.
21. NAC, Borden, Microfilm C-4345, p 65843B.
22. 21 January 1922, Wigley, p 154, footnote 28.
23. Borden, *Canadian Constitutional Studies,* p 130.
24. Dawson, pp 54–5.
25. *DCER*, Vol 3, 1919–1925, p 74.
26. *DCER*, Vol 3, 1919–1925, p 80.

27. R M Dawson, *William Lyon Mackenzie King: A Political Biography, Vol 1, 1874–1923* (Methuen & Co Ltd, London: 1958) p 408.
28. *DCER*, Vol 3, 1919–1925, pp 74–5.
29. 11 October 1922, *DCER*, Vol 3, 1919–1925, pp 82–3.
30. Eayrs, p 13.
31. *DCER*, Vol 3, 1919–1925, p 239.
32. 8 October 1923, *DCER*, Vol 3, 1919–1925, p 237.
33. 15 October 1923, *DCER*, Vol 3, 1919–1925, p 251.
34. *DCER*, Vol 3, 1919–1925, p 256.
35. *DCER*, Vol 3, 1919–1925, p 256.

7: Final Years: The Aftermath of the Peace Conference

1. http://www.dfait-maeci.gc.ca/department/history.
2. *DCER*, Vol 3, 1919–25, p 138.
3. Austin Chamberlain and Charles Dawes received the Nobel Peace Prize in 1925, Gustav Stresemann and Aristide Briand in 1926.
4. http://avalon.law.yale.edu/20th_century/locarno.
5. Dawson, p 103.
6. Brown, *Borden,* p 199.
7. Wigley, p 252.
8. Wigley, p 252.
9. Wigley, p 263.
10. Wigley, p 264.
11. Wigley, p 271.
12. J C Beaglehole, 'The British Commonwealth of Nations', in C L Mowat (ed), *The New Cambridge Modern History,* Vol XII (Cambridge University Press, Cambridge: 1968) p 386.
13. Soward, p 15.
14. Saunders, p 62.

15. *The Times*, 29 August 1930, p 12.
16. *The Times*, 11 June 1937, pp 16–18.
17. *The Times*, 11 June 1937, p 16.

8: Peace and War: Canada's Place in World Affairs

1. Brown in Granatstein, *Towards a New World*, p 30.
2. Borden, *Canadian Constitutional Studies*, p 138.
3. Borden, *Canadian Constitutional Studies*, p 139.
4. N Mansergh, *The Commonwealth Experience*, p 272.
5. Hillmer and Granatstein, p 126.
6. R Borden, *Letters to Limbo* (University of Toronto Press, Toronto: 1971) p 269.
7. Hillmer and Granatstein, pp 145–6.
8. Hillmer and Granatstein, p 154.
9. M Thornton, 'Strained Relations? Canada and Britain and the Restructuring of the Post-War World, 1943–1949', in R Haar and N Wynn (eds), *Transatlantic Conflict and Consensus: Culture, History and Politics* (Cambridge Academic, Cambridge: 2009), pp 91–111.
10. J W Holmes, 'Canadian External Policies Since 1945', *International Journal*, Vol XVIII, No 2, Spring 1963, pp 142–3.
11. Stacey, p 287.

Conclusion

1. Borden, *Letters to Limbo*, p 269.
2. Borden, *Letters to Limbo*, p 270.
3. English in MacKenzie, p 78.
4. Borden, *Memoirs*, Vol 2, p 1044.

Chronology

YEAR	AGE	THE LIFE AND THE LAND
1854		26 June: Robert Laird Borden born in Grand Pré, Nova Scotia.
1863	9	Joins Acacia Villa School, Nova Scotia.
1867	12	Confederation of Canada.
1869	14	March: becomes an assistant teacher at Acacia Villa School.
1873	19	Moves to teach at Glenwood Institute in Matawan, New Jersey, United States.
1874	20	August: returns to Nova Scotia and is apprenticed to the law firm of Weatherbe and Graham.
1878	24	Admitted to the Nova Scotia Bar, although he had passed his examinations the previous year.
1882	28	Joins the law firm of Graham and Tupper as a junior partner.
1887	33	Appears before the Supreme Court of Canada.
1889	35	25 September: Marries Laura Bond from Halifax, Nova Scotia. Forms the law firm of Borden, Ritchie, Parker and Chisholm.

YEAR	HISTORY	CULTURE
1854	Crimean War: Britain and France ally with Ottoman Empire; landings in the Crimea, siege of Sebastopol begins.	Alfred Lord Tennyson, *The Charge of the Light Brigade*. Henry David Thoreau, *Walden, or Life in the Woods*.
1863	US Civil War; Lincoln's 'Gettysburg Address'	Charles Kingsley, *The Water Babies*.
1867	South African diamond fields discovered.	Anthony Trollope, *The Last Chronicle of Barset*.
1869	Red River rebellion begins in Canada.	Mark Twain, *The Innocents Abroad*.
1873	Republic proclaimed in Spain.	Leo Tolstoy, *Anna Karenina*.
1874	Britain annexes Fiji Islands.	Thomas Hardy, *Far from the Madding Crowd*.
1878	Russo-Turkish War: armistice signed. Congress of Berlin discusses Eastern Question.	Thomas Hardy, *The Return of the Native*. Algernon Charles Swinburne, *Poems and Ballads*.
1882	Triple Alliance between Italy, Germany and Austria-Hungary.	Leslie Stephen, *Science of Ethics*. Richard Wagner, *Parsifal*.
1887	First Colonial Conference in London.	Vincent Van Gogh, *Moulin de la Galette*.
1889	London Dock Strike. Austro-Hungarian Crown Prince Rudolf commits suicide at Mayerling.	Jerome K Jerome, *Three Men in a Boat*. Richard Strauss, *Don Juan*.

YEAR	AGE	THE LIFE AND THE LAND
1893	39	Appears in front of the Judicial Committee of the Privy Council in England.
1896	42	Agrees to stand as a Member of Parliament for Halifax. 23 June: wins seat in the general election.
1899	45	Outbreak of Second Boer War, Canada sends volunteer troops.
1900	46	March: father dies. 7 November: re-elected to Parliament.
1901	47	Becomes Leader of the Conservative Party.
1904	50	3 November: defeated in the general election. Liberal Party under Wilfrid Laurier forms a Government.
1905	51	4 February: Elected to Parliament.
1908	54	26 October: Liberal Party under Wilfrid Laurier wins the general election.
1911	57	21 September: elected to Parliament. Conservative Party wins the general election: becomes Prime Minister.
1913	59	Emergency Naval Aid Bill rejected by the Canadian Senate.
1914	60	Awarded GCMG by King George V. Emergency War legislation introduced. 3 October: Canadian Expeditionary Force sails for England.

YEAR	HISTORY	CULTURE
1893	Franco-Russian alliance signed. British House of Lords rejects second Irish Home Rule Bill.	Art Nouveau appears in Europe. Giacomo Puccini, *Manon Lescaut*.
1896	Jameson Raid fails in Transvaal: German Kaiser Wilhelm II sends 'Kruger Telegram'.	Anton Chekhov, *The Seagull*.
1899	Second Boer War begins.	Edward Elgar, *Enigma Variations*.
1900	US President William McKinley re-elected.	Joseph Conrad, *Lord Jim*.
1901	Britain's Queen Victoria dies: Edward VII becomes King.	Pablo Picasso's 'Blue Period' begins.
1904	Russo-Japanese War begins. Theodore Roosevelt elected US President.	Sigmund Freud, *The Psychopathology of Everyday Life*.
1905	Anglo-Japanese alliance renewed.	Claude Debussy, *La Mer*.
1908	William Howard Taft elected US President.	Marc Chagall, *Nu Rouge*.
1911	German gunboat *Panther* arrives in Agadir: triggers international crisis.	D H Lawrence, *The White Peacock*. Saki (H H Munro), *The Chronicles of Clovis*.
1913	London Ambassadors Conference ends 1st Balkan War: establishes independent Albania. Second Balkan War.	Marcel Proust, *Du côté de chez Swann*. Igor Stravinsky, *Le Sacre du Printemps*.
1914	First World War begins; Battles of Mons, the Marne and First Ypres.	James Joyce, *Dubliners*. Gustav Holst, *The Planets*.

YEAR	AGE	THE LIFE AND THE LAND
1915	61	Makes first wartime visits to France and Britain. Attends a British Cabinet meeting at the invitation of Prime Minister Asquith. March: Mother dies.
1916	62	Fire engulfs the Parliament building in Ottawa; life of Canadian Parliament extended for a year.
1917	63	Attends the Imperial War Cabinet and Imperial War Conference. Resolution IX introduced at the Imperial War Conference. 18 May: presents his policy of conscription to the Canadian Parliament. Creates a coalition Government (Unionist) in the hope of maintaining national unity. 20 September: Wartime Elections Act passed in Parliament. 12 October: forms a Unionist Government. 5 December: Halifax disaster. 17 December: elected to Parliament and forms a Unionist Government.
1918	64	Conscription eventually introduced in Canada. Attends the Imperial War Cabinet and Imperial Conference in London. 11 November: learns of the armistice aboard the *Mauritania* sailing for England.

YEAR	HISTORY	CULTURE
1915	First World War: Battles of Neuve Chapelle and Loos, 'Shells Scandal', Gallipoli campaign. Sinking of the *Lusitania*.	John Buchan, *The Thirty-Nine Steps.* Max Reger, *Mozart Variations.* Film: *The Birth of a Nation.*
1916	First World War: Battles of Verdun, the Somme and Jutland.	Henri Matisse, *The Three Sisters.* Claude Monet, *Waterlilies.*
1917	First World War: Battle of Passchendaele (Third Ypres); British and Commonwealth forces take Jerusalem; USA declares war on Germany. February Revolution in Russia. Balfour Declaration favouring establishment of national home for Jewish People in Palestine. German and Russian delegates sign armistice at Brest-Litovsk.	P G Wodehouse, *The Man With Two Left Feet.* T S Eliot, *Prufrock and Other Observations.* Leon Feuchtwanger, *Jud Suess.* Piet Mondrian launches *De Stijl* magazine in Holland. Sergei Prokofiev, *Classical Symphony.* Film: *Easy Street.*
1918	Armistice signed between Allies and Germany; German Fleet surrenders. Kaiser Wilhelm of Germany abdicates.	Gerard Manley Hopkins, *Poems.* Luigi Pirandello, *Six Characters in Search of an Author.*

YEAR	AGE	THE LIFE AND THE LAND
1919	65	11 January: leaves London for Paris and the Peace Conference. Attempts to amend Article X of the Covenant of the League of Nations. 14 May: leaves Paris and returns to Ottawa via England. Charles Doherty and Arthur Sifton sign the Treaty of Versailles for Canada. 16 December: offers his resignation to Cabinet, but is persuaded to stay on temporarily.
1920	66	10 July: finally resigns as Prime Minister of Canada and is replaced by Arthur Meighen.
1921	67	Represents Canada on the British Empire Delegation at the Washington Naval Disarmament Conference. 13 December: signs Four-Power Treaty at the Washington Conference.
1922	68	6 February: signs Nine-Power Treaty and Five-Power Treaty at the Washington Conference. October: gives Marfleet lectures at the University of Toronto. Chanak Crisis is an embarrassment in Canadian-British Empire relations.
1924	70	Dawes Plan approved.
1925	71	Locarno Pact.
1926	72	Imperial Conference of 1926 and Balfour Declaration develop definition of the British Commonwealth and reflect Borden's earlier efforts.

YEAR	HISTORY	CULTURE
1919	Benito Mussolini founds Fascist movement in Italy. Irish War of Independence begins. US Senate vetoes ratification of Versailles Treaty leaving US outside League of Nations.	George Bernard Shaw, *Heartbreak House.* Eugene D'Albert, *Revolutionshochzeit.* Edward Elgar, *Concerto in E Minor for Cello.* Film: *The Cabinet of Dr Caligari.*
1920	Warren G Harding wins US Presidential election. Bolsheviks win Russian Civil War.	F Scott Fitzgerald, *This Side of Paradise.* Katherine Mansfield, *Bliss.*
1921	Paris Conference of wartime allies fixes Germany's reparation payments. Irish Free State established. Peace treaty signed between Russia and Germany.	Aldous Huxley, *Chrome Yellow.* Georges Braque, *Still Life with Guitar.* Max Ernst, *The Elephant Celebes.*
1922	Election in Irish Free State gives majority to Pro-Treaty candidates: IRA takes large areas under its control. League of Nations Council approves British Mandate in Palestine.	T S Eliot, *The Waste Land.* James Joyce, *Ulysses.* F Scott Fitzgerald, *The Beautiful and Damned.* BBC founded.
1924	German Nazi Party wins 32 seats in Reichstag.	Thomas Mann, *The Magic Mountain.*
1925	Hindenberg elected President of Germany.	Film: *Battleship Potemkin.*
1926	General Strike in Britain.	Franz Kafka, *The Castle.* A A Milne, *Winnie the Pooh.*

YEAR	AGE	THE LIFE AND THE LAND
1927	73	Gives Rhodes lectures at the University of Oxford.
1930	76	Leads the Canadian delegation to the League of Nations.
1931	77	11 December. Statute of Westminster formally defines the British Commonwealth of Nations. Manchurian Crisis becomes a problem for the League of Nations.
1935	81	Abyssinian crisis leads to a confusing policy by Canada at the League of Nations. Borden pessimistic about the prospect for the maintenance of European peace.
1937	82	10 June: Dies at home in Ottawa.

YEAR	HISTORY	CULTURE
1927	India Commission established to review Montagu-Chelmsford Act.	Virginia Woolf, *To the Lighthouse.* Adolf Hitler, *Mein Kampf.*
1930	London Naval Treaty.	W H Auden, *Poems.*
1931	Britain abandons Gold Standard. National Government formed in Britain.	Salvador Dali, *The Persistence of Memory.* Max Beckmann, *Still Life with Studio Window.*
1935	Hoare-Laval Pact. Hitler announces anti-Jewish 'Nuremberg Laws'.	Ivy Compton-Burnett, *A House and its Head.* Films: *The 39 Steps. Top Hat.*
1937	Japan invades China.	Jean-Paul Sartre, *Nausea.*

Further Reading

Robert Laird Borden produced two volumes of memoirs, *Robert Laird Borden: His Memoirs* (The Macmillan Company of Canada Ltd, Toronto: 1938), books that are not entirely self-revealing, but they do establish the statesman that Borden himself wished to present. Edited by his nephew and published after Borden's death, they provide a rather staid but detailed account of Robert Borden's political life; I found them much more revealing on a second reading. The oddity that is *Letters to Limbo* (only published in 1971 by University of Toronto Press, Toronto) reveals Borden's literary ambitions as he invented a newspaper, the *Limbo Recorder and Guardian*, which allowed him to express personal feelings previously kept quiet because of his political duties and acceptance of the importance of self-control. As world crises developed in the 1930s so did Robert Borden's pessimism; just before his death he anticipated that at some point in the near future there would be another European war.

Borden's constitutional interests are evident in the delivery of the Marfleet Lectures at the University of Toronto, published in 1922 as *Canadian Constitutional Studies* (Oxford University Press, London: 1922), and his Rhodes Memorial

Lectures at the University of Oxford, published as *Canada in the Commonwealth* (Clarendon Press, Oxford: 1929). These are scholarly pieces on the international status of Canada and Canada's relationship to Great Britain in foreign policy matters.

Manuscript sources for Borden are housed at the National Archives of Canada in Ottawa and comprise a very large collection of Borden's papers (most are duplicated on microfilm). An electronic database at the National Archives of Canada contains an inventory of the personal papers of the Canadian Prime Ministers from John A Macdonald to Pierre E Trudeau. *The Borden Papers, 1893–1937* run to 129 reels of microfilm, of which a lot of the OC series (put together by W F O'Connor) are background material collected for his *Memoirs*. From this OC series, the manuscript series MG 26 Volume 119 contains material on the Washington Naval Conference in 1921 and 1922. A series listed as 'Borden, Sir Robert L, Fonds' contains notes on the Paris Peace Conference. Borden's papers have been available since 1952, but should still have some interest for new researchers who may wish to evaluate Borden in a different light. Theses continue to be written on Canadian political, social and economic areas in the early 20th century. It is testament to Borden that they are also written on his role in Canadian international affairs.

On the Paris Peace Conference, there are excellent published documents based around individual countries. On a par with the excellent series *Foreign Relations of the United States* and *Documents on British Foreign Policy* is the Canadian equivalent *Documents on Canadian External Relations*. Volume 2 (Queen's Printer, Ottawa: 1969) deals with the Paris Peace Conference of 1919 and was edited by R A MacKay of Carleton University. Lovell C Clark of the University of Manitoba edited Volume 3 dealing with 1919–25, a collection that runs to 1,007 pages.

The main biography of Robert Borden is the two-volume work of Robert Craig Brown (The Macmillan Company of Canada Ltd, Toronto), published in 1975 and 1980. It is a major achievement, drawing on excellent manuscript sources and published records. No doubt this work has put off other scholars attempting to publish further substantial biographies of him.

On the Commonwealth, a number of excellent and now standard texts have appeared over the past 45 years. Robert MacGregor Dawson's *The Development of Dominion Status, 1900–1936* (Frank Cass & Co, London: 1965) covers very effectively Dominion attitudes towards imperial affairs and in particular the topics of imperial defence and the imperial conferences. It is an edited work including over 300 pages of documents. *Britain and the Commonwealth Alliance 1918–1939* by R F Holland (Macmillan, London: 1981) deals with interesting issues of not only the formation of the Commonwealth, but also the Dominions Office and the Locarno Pact as well as the Commonwealth and economic crisis of the Great Depression. A book that takes an even more global look at Britain's imperial interests is W David McIntyre's *The Commonwealth of Nations; Origins and Impact, 1869–1971* (University of Minnesota Press, Minneapolis: 1977). It almost goes without saying that Cambridge historian Nicholas Mansergh's *The Commonwealth Experience* (Weidenfeld and Nicolson, London: 1969) has been required reading since its publication. J D B Miller from Australia produced a book on the 'Old Commonwealth', *Britain and the Old Dominions* (Chatto & Windus, London: 1966). The phrase 'New

Commonwealth' has come to be used by many authors from 1947 onwards, including David McIntyre in *Colonies into Commonwealth* (Blandford Press, London: 1966), as a phrase covering the period when British Empire colonies choose to join the Commonwealth as independent nations.

I will not discuss further or recommend any of the excellent works on the Paris Peace Conference settlements by Alan Sharp, Mike Dockrill, Sally Marks and A Lentin. Their works and others are listed and covered by other books in this 'Makers of the Modern World' series. A footnote in Borden's *Memoirs* criticised Foreign Office official Harold Nicolson's memoir, *Peacemaking 1919* (Constable, London: 1933). *Nicholson (sic),* he wrote, *a very clever young man, has written a most interesting, but rather unreliable account of the Peace Conference. In reading his narrative, 'Peacemaking', I thought of a mirror that gives a distorted reflection. As an illustration of the imperfections of his narrative, he fails to mention General Botha who was a commanding figure at the Peace Conference. In truth his history recounts only his own experience, although its title conveys a much wider impression* (R L Borden, *Memoirs*, Vol 2, p 909). A book that does mention Botha and Borden is the award-winning *Peacemakers: The Paris Conference of 1919 and Its Attempt to End War* by Professor Margaret MacMillan (John Murray, London: 2001). This may be the one single volume that students choose to read about the six months at Paris for some time to come.

Although much is now written about Canadian peacekeeping for the United Nations and the crises in Palestine, Korea, Suez, Congo and the Lebanon among others, far less attention has been paid to the League of Nations and Canada. Obvious reasons exist for this discrepancy in coverage, particularly since the League's failures or inactivity are often highlighted as contributing towards the outbreak of the Second World War, and Canada's opposition to Article X does them no favours in this debate. Richard Veatch's book, *Canada and the League of Nations* (University of Toronto Press, Toronto: 1975), however, covers this story in considerable detail and manages to develop a higher profile for Canada at the League of Nations than most historians of the period have managed.

Bibliography

Unpublished sources

Sir Robert L Borden Papers, National Archives of Canada, Ottawa, OC series, Fonds (microfilm)

Lloyd George Papers, House of Lords Record Office, London

Published official documents

Documents on Canadian External Relations, Vol 1, 1909–1918 (Queen's Printer, Ottawa: 1967)

R A MacKay (ed), *Documents on Canadian External Relations, Vol 2, The Paris Peace Conference of 1919* (Queen's Printer, Ottawa: 1969)

L C Clark (ed), *Documents on Canadian External Relations, Vol 3, 1919–1925* (Information Canada, Ottawa: 1970)

Published diaries, letters, memoirs and speeches

H Borden (ed), *Robert Laird Borden: His Memoirs,* Vols 1 and 2 (The Macmillan Company of Canada Ltd, Toronto: 1938)

R L Borden, *Letters to Limbo* (University of Toronto Press, Toronto: 1971)

R L Borden, *Canadian Constitutional Studies: The Marfleet Lectures, University of Toronto, October 1921* (Oxford University Press, London: 1922)

R L Borden, *Canada in the Commonwealth* (Clarendon Press, Oxford: 1929)

R L Borden and J C Smuts, *The Empire and the War: The Voice of the Dominions* (The Empire Parliamentary Association, London: 1917)

R Cecil, Viscount Cecil of Chelwood, *All the Way* (Hodder and Stoughton Ltd, London: 1949)

W M Hughes, *The Splendid Adventure* (Ernest Benn, London: 1929)

D Lloyd George, *War Memoirs,* Vol IV (Odhams, London: 1934)

D Lloyd George, *Memoirs of the Peace Conference,* Vol 1 (Yale University Press, New Haven: 1939)

Biographies

R Bothwell, *Loring Christie: the Failure of Bureaucratic Imperialism* (Garland Publishing, New York: 1988)

R C Brown, *Robert Laird Borden: A Biography, Vol 1, 1854–1914* (The Macmillan Company of Canada Ltd, Toronto: 1975)

R C Brown, *Robert Laird Borden: A Biography, Vol 2, 1914–1937* (The Macmillan Company of Canada Ltd, Toronto: 1980)

R M Dawson, *William Lyon Mackenzie King: A Political Biography, Vol 1, 1874–1923* (Methuen & Co Ltd, London: 1958)

J English, *Borden: His Life and World* (McGraw-Hill Ryerson, Toronto: 1977)

H Purcell, *Lloyd George* (Haus Publishing, London: 2006)

K Saunders, *Robert Borden* (Fitzhenry and Whiteside Ltd, Ontario: 1978)

A Sharp, *David Lloyd George: Great Britain* (Haus Publishing, London: 2008)

Other secondary sources

R Bothwell, I M Drummond and J English, *Canada, 1900–1945* (University of Toronto Press, Toronto: 1987)

G L Cook, 'Sir Robert Borden, Lloyd George and British Military Policy, 1917–18,' *The Historical Journal*, Vol XIV, No 2 (June 1971)

R M Dawson, *The Development of Dominion Status, 1900–1936* (Frank Cass & Co, London: 1965)

M L Dockrill and Z Steiner, 'The Foreign Office and the Paris Peace Conference in 1919', *International History Review*, Vol 11, No 1 (1980)

M L Dockrill and J Fisher (eds.), *The Paris Peace Conference, 1919* (Palgrave, Basingstoke: 2001)

I M Drummond, *Imperial Economic Policy, 1917–1939* (Allen and Unwin, London: 1974)

J Eayrs, *In Defence of Canada: From the Great War to the Great Depression* (University of Toronto Press, Toronto: 1967)

C C Eldridge (ed), *Kith and Kin: Canada, Britain and the United States from the Revolution to the Cold War* (University of Wales Press, Cardiff: 1997)

J English, *The Decline of Politics: the Conservatives and the Party System, 1901–1920* (University of Toronto Press, Toronto: 1977)

J L Granatstein, *The Ottawa Men: The Civil Service Mandarins, 1935–1957* (Oxford University Press, Toronto: 1982)

J L Granatstein, *Towards a New World: Readings in the History of Canadian Foreign Policy* (Copp Clark Pitman, Toronto: 1992)

J F Hilliker, *Canada's Department of External Affairs, Vol 1, The Early Years 1909–1946* (McGill-Queen's University Press, Montreal: 1990)

N Hillmer (ed), *Partners Nevertheless: Canadian-American Relations in the Twentieth Century* (Copp Clark Pitman, Toronto: 1989)

N Hillmer and J L Granatstein, *Empire to Umpire: Canada and the World to the 1990s* (Copp Clark Longman Ltd, Toronto: 1994)

R F Holland, *Britain and the Commonwealth Alliance, 1918–1939* (Macmillan, London: 1981)

J W Holmes, 'Canadian External Policies Since 1945', *International Journal*, Vol XVIII, No 2 (Spring 1963)

B Hutchison, *Mr Prime Minister, 1867–1964* (Harcourt, Brace and World Inc, New York: 1964)

P Lyon (ed), *Britain and Canada: Survey of a Changing Relationship* (Cass, London: 1976)

D MacKenzie (ed), *Canada and the First World War: Essays in Honour of Robert Craig Brown* (University of Toronto Press, Toronto: 2005)

M MacMillan, *Peacemakers: The Paris Peace Conference of 1919 and Its Attempt to End War* (John Murray, London: 2001)

N Mansergh, *The Commonwealth Experience* (Weidenfeld and Nicolson, London: 1969)

W D McIntyre, *The Commonwealth of Nations: Origins and Impact, 1869–1971* (University of Minnesota Press, Minneapolis: 1977)

W D McIntyre, *Colonies into Commonwealth* (Blanford Press, London: 1966)
J D B Miller, *Britain and the Old Dominions* (Chatto & Windus, London: 1966)
C L Mowat (ed), *The New Cambridge Modern History, Vol XII, The Shifting Balance of World Forces 1898–1945* (Cambridge University Press, Cambridge: 1968)
L Oppenheim, *International Law: A Treatise, Vol 1, Peace* (8th edition; Longmans, Green, London: 1955)
M Schmoeckel, 'The Internationalist as a Scientist and Herald: Lassa Oppenheim,' *European Journal of International Law*, Vol 11, No 3 (2000)
A Sharp, *The Versailles Settlement: Peacemaking in Paris, 1919* (Macmillan, Basingstoke: 1991)
A Siegfried, *Canada: An International Power* (Arno Press, New York: 1972)
C P Stacey, *Canada and the Age of Conflict: A History of Canadian External Policies* (The Macmillan Company of Canada Ltd, Toronto: 1977)
C P Stacey, *Mackenzie King and the Atlantic Triangle* (The Macmillan Company of Canada Ltd, Toronto: 1976)
P D Stevens (ed), *The 1911 General Election* (Copp Clark Publishing Co, Toronto: 1970)
H W V Temperley (ed.), *A History of the Peace Conference of Paris,* Vol VI (Oxford University Press, London: 1969)
A J Toynbee, *British Commonwealth Relations: Proceedings of the First Unofficial Conference at Toronto, September 1933* (Oxford University Press, London: 1934)
M Thornton, 'Strained Relations? Canada and Britain and the Restructuring of the Post-War World, 1943–1949', in R Haar and N Wynn (eds), *Transatlantic Conflict and*

Consensus: Culture, History and Politics (Cambridge Academic, Cambridge: 2009)

R Veatch, *Canada and the League of Nations* (University of Toronto Press, Toronto: 1975)

P G Wigley, *Canada and the Transition to Commonwealth: British-Canadian Relations 1917–1926* (Cambridge University Press, Cambridge: 1977)

Picture Sources

The author and publishers wish to express their thanks to the following sources of illustrative material and/or permission to reproduce it. They will make proper acknowledgements in future editions in the event that any omissions have occurred.

Illustrations courtesy of Topham Picturepoint.

Endpapers

The Signing of Peace in the Hall of Mirrors, Versailles, 28th June 1919 by Sir William Orpen (Imperial War Museum: Bridgeman Art Library)
Front row: Dr Johannes Bell (Germany) signing with Herr Hermann Müller leaning over him
Middle row (seated, left to right): General Tasker H Bliss, Col E M House, Mr Henry White, Mr Robert Lansing, President Woodrow Wilson (United States); M Georges Clemenceau (France); Mr David Lloyd George, Mr Andrew Bonar Law, Mr Arthur J Balfour, Viscount Milner, Mr G N Barnes (Great Britain); Prince Saionji (Japan)
Back row (left to right): M Eleftherios Venizelos (Greece);

Dr Afonso Costa (Portugal); Lord Riddell (British Press); Sir George E Foster (Canada); M Nikola Pašić (Serbia); M Stephen Pichon (France); Col Sir Maurice Hankey, Mr Edwin S Montagu (Great Britain); the Maharajah of Bikaner (India); Signor Vittorio Emanuele Orlando (Italy); M Paul Hymans (Belgium); General Louis Botha (South Africa); Mr W M Hughes (Australia)

Jacket images

(Front): Imperial War Museum: akg Images.
(Back): *Peace Conference at the Quai d'Orsay* by Sir William Orpen (Imperial War Museum: akg Images).
Left to right (seated): Signor Orlando (Italy); Mr Robert Lansing, President Woodrow Wilson (United States); M Georges Clemenceau (France); Mr David Lloyd George, Mr Andrew Bonar Law, Mr Arthur J Balfour (Great Britain);
Left to right (standing): M Paul Hymans (Belgium); Mr Eleftherios Venizelos (Greece); The Emir Feisal (The Hashemite Kingdom); Mr W F Massey (New Zealand); General Jan Smuts (South Africa); Col E M House (United States); General Louis Botha (South Africa); Prince Saionji (Japan); Mr W M Hughes (Australia); Sir Robert Borden (Canada); Mr G N Barnes (Great Britain); M Ignacy Paderewski (Poland)

Index

A

Alaska 6, 10
Anglo-French treaty (1919) 88
Amery, Leopold 49, 129
Asquith, Herbert 33, 44, 47–8, 67, 98
Atlantic Ocean 6–7, 9, 28, 48
Australia xi, 9, 12–13, 49, 65–6, 69, 72, 87, 103, 106, 113–14, 121, 139
Austria 37, 88

B

Balfour, Arthur J xiii, 14, 51, 87, 98, 100, 103–4, 122, 127–9
Belgium 7, 22, 66, 71, 80, 104, 124–6
Bennett, Robert Bedford 35, 44–5, 136–7
Black Sea 112, 114
Bonar Law, Andrew xiii, 29, 45, 115
Borden family 17, 19, 21
Borden, Laura Bond 20, 29, 39, 133
Borden, Sir Robert
- birth xi, 17
- Canadian politics, and xii, 28–35, 97–133, 135–143, 145
- character and appearance ix–x, 16–17, 144, 146–7
- death xi
- early life and career 16–27

Paris Peace Conference, and 37–93
Botha, General Louis 84, 175
British Columbia 7, 21, 26, 75, 120
Byng, Sir Julian Hedworth George 127–8

C

Canada
First World War, and ix–x, xii, 8–9, 11–12, 14–15, 23, 35, 39–61, 79, 89–91, 97–8, 116, 132, 134, 140, 143–4, 146
Paris Peace Conference, and xii–iii, 10, 13, 15, 26, 37–93, 97–8, 103–4, 109, 128, 135, 142, 144, 146
Post-war history 97–143
Pre-war history 1–15, 23–35
Cecil, Lord Robert xiii, 67, 75, 77–8
Chanak Crisis 10, 48, 111–16, 126
China 104, 117, 135
Christie, Loring Cheney xiii, 31–2, 41, 69, 103
Churchill, Winston 32–3, 58, 112–15, 141–2
Clemenceau, Georges xiii, 72, 76, 80, 83, 87, 91
Conservative Party (Canadian) xi, 19–22, 25–6, 30–2, 34, 45, 49, 55, 68, 105, 115, 136
Czechoslovakia 125, 139

D

Dandurand, Raoul 9, 122–3, 131
Dawes Plan 123–4
Doherty, Charles Joseph 69, 80–2, 85, 87, 100

F

First World War ix–x, xii, 8–9, 11–12, 14–15, 23, 35, 39–61, 79, 89–91, 97–8, 116, 132, 134, 140, 143–4, 146
Foster, Sir George E x, xiii, 24, 68–71, 80, 85
France 4, 7, 20, 44, 65–6, 70, 72, 74, 80, 82, 87, 90, 104, 106–7, 112, 116, 123–5, 130, 132, 140

G

Gordon, Sir Charles Blair 110
Greece 73, 112

H

Harris, Lloyd 79
Hillmer, Norman 32, 60, 140
Hitler, Adolf 138–9
Hughes, Charles Evans 106
Hughes, Colonel Sam 43–4
Hughes, William Morris (Billy) 49, 65–6

I

Imperial Conferences 47, 116–21, 127–30, 138
India 12–13, 48, 51, 66–7, 69, 72, 86, 103, 112, 116, 125
Italy 65, 70, 74, 87, 104, 106, 112, 124–6, 136–8, 145

J

Japan 34, 70, 77–8, 91, 104–9, 117, 120, 135, 138, 145

K

Kemp, Sir Edward 88
Kerr, Philip 52
Kipling, Rudyard 23–4

L

Lansing, Robert xiii, 71, 78–9
Laurier, Sir Wilfrid 8, 22–3, 25–6, 29–32, 34, 40, 47, 53–5, 115, 118, 146
League of Nations 3, 6, 9, 11–12, 15, 50, 67–8, 74–5, 77–8, 80–1, 83, 88, 91, 93, 99–102, 110–11, 120, 122–3, 126, 128, 131–2, 135–9, 142, 144, 145
Lloyd George, David xiii, 10, 33, 45, 47–8, 50, 52, 54, 56, 59–60, 67, 69–72, 74–6, 78, 80, 84, 86–9, 91–2, 98–9, 102–4, 110, 112–15, 117, 128, 146

M

Mackenzie King, William L xiii, 11, 32, 92, 105, 107–8, 110, 113–21, 123, 126–8, 134, 137, 139–41, 143
Manitoba 7, 26
Meighen, Arthur xiii, 32,

45, 68, 103, 105–6, 115, 117, 128, 133
Milner, Lord 52, 87–8

N

New Brunswick 7, 68
New Zealand 9, 13, 72, 103, 113–14, 139
Northwest Territories 7
Nova Scotia xi–xiii, 7, 16–21, 26, 84, 143

O

Ontario 7, 18, 26, 39, 43, 68, 131
Oppenheim, Lassa 11–12, 41

P

Palestine 14, 128
Paris Peace Conference xii–iii, 10, 13, 15, 26, 37–93, 97–8, 103–4, 109, 128, 135, 142, 144, 146
Pearson, Lester B xiii, 17, 141–2
Perley, Sir George Halsey 45
Poland 125, 139
Pope, Sir Joseph xii, 5–6, 31
Prince Edward Island 7

Q

Quebec 4–5, 7, 23, 28, 30–1, 42, 45, 53, 68, 123, 131, 137

R

Riddell, Walter A 136–7
Russia 7, 53, 57–8, 73, 105, 112

S

Second World War 9, 11, 14, 53, 59, 92, 134, 139–43, 145
Serbia x, 69, 79–80
Sifton, Arthur L x, xiii, 68–9, 77, 85, 87
Smuts, Jan Christian xiii, 51–2, 74, 78, 90, 103
South Africa 9, 13, 27, 51–2, 67, 69, 72, 75, 84, 103, 113, 127, 139
Soward, Frederic H 59, 90
Stacey, Charles x, 28, 34, 61, 64, 89, 143

T

Tupper, Sir Charles 19–21, 24, 118
Turkey 10, 48, 58, 88, 98, 111–12, 115–16

U

United States 4–6, 9, 11, 15, 18, 23, 30–1, 50, 53, 70–6, 89–90, 99–104, 106–8, 111, 117–20, 123–4, 136–7, 140–2, 145

W

White, Sir Thomas 61, 64–5, 85
Wilson, Woodrow xiii, 10, 50, 61, 70–2, 80–1, 87, 100
Wrong, Hume 17, 141–2

UK PUBLICATION: November 2008 to December 2010
CLASSIFICATION: Biography/History/
International Relations
FORMAT: 198 × 128mm
EXTENT: 208pp
ILLUSTRATIONS: 6 photographs plus 4 maps
TERRITORY: world

Chronology of life in context, full index, bibliography innovative layout with sidebars

Woodrow Wilson: United States of America by Brian Morton
Friedrich Ebert: Germany by Harry Harmer
Georges Clemenceau: France by David Watson
David Lloyd George: Great Britain by Alan Sharp
Prince Saionji: Japan by Jonathan Clements
Wellington Koo: China by Jonathan Clements
Eleftherios Venizelos: Greece by Andrew Dalby
From the Sultan to Atatürk: Turkey by Andrew Mango
The Hashemites: The Dream of Arabia by Robert McNamara
Chaim Weizmann: The Dream of Zion by Tom Fraser
Piip, Meierovics & Voldemaras: Estonia, Latvia & Lithuania by Charlotte Alston
Ignacy Paderewski: Poland by Anita Prazmowska
Beneš, Masaryk: Czechoslovakia by Peter Neville
Károlyi & Bethlen: Hungary by Bryan Cartledge
Karl Renner: Austria by Jamie Bulloch
Vittorio Orlando: Italy by Spencer Di Scala
Pašić & Trumbić: The Kingdom of Serbs, Croats and Slovenes by Dejan Djokic
Aleksandŭr Stamboliĭski: Bulgaria by R J Crampton
Ion Bratianu: Romania by Keith Hitchin
Paul Hymans: Belgium by Sally Marks
General Smuts: South Africa by Antony Lentin
William Hughes: Australia by Carl Bridge
William Massey: New Zealand by James Watson
Sir Robert Borden: Canada by Martin Thornton
Maharajah of Bikaner: India by Hugh Purcell
Afonso Costa: Portugal by Filipe Ribeiro de Meneses
Epitácio Pessoa: Brazil by Michael Streeter
South America by Michael Streeter
Central America by Michael Streeter
South East Asia by Andrew Dalby
The League of Nations by Ruth Henig
Consequences of Peace: The Versailles Settlement – Aftermath and Legacy by Alan Sharp